WITHDRAWN

The Art of Bertolt Brecht

THE ART OF

Bertolt Brecht

By *WALTER WEIDELI*

English version by Daniel Russell

NEW YORK UNIVERSITY PRESS   1963

The original French edition of this book appeared under the title Brecht *and was published by Editions Universitaires, Paris.*

CONTENTS

v

The Art of Bertolt Brecht

1 · The Old and the New

> For our era, and that of our children, is the
> era of combat between the old and the new,
> and these combats rage within the innermost
> part of each one of us.
>
> GEDICHTE AUS DEM MESSINGKAUF

IT IS TOO OFTEN BELIEVED that Hitlerism was only an accident
in the history of the German people. Actually, it marks the ex-
plosive victory of pernicious tendencies that had been developing
for a long time. Their beginnings are to be found at the dawn
of the nineteenth century in the restless birth of the industrial
age. The failure of the bourgeois revolution in Germany, the
careful perfection of an immense bureaucratic machinery, the
political fragmentation of the country, the reinforcement of the
feudal institutions: all these things only accentuated the nar-
rowness, the ignorance, and the philistine passivity against which
the German intellectuals of the age of reason had unceasingly
protested. The attitude of the whole romantic generation which
followed that of Weimar permits us to fathom the stifling
misery of the times. Unfulfilled in their deep need for a harmonious society, these writers took refuge in the dreamy, irrational, yes even sickly, part of themselves, in that night of
instinct which Novalis eulogized. Blind and alone, they idealize
precisely that which mutilates and oppresses them. Their
anarchical revolt finally becomes a servile respect for authority.

It seems necessary to me to recall these things, for they enable
us to unearth a veritable mechanism of self-destruction, which
perpetuated itself throughout the imperial era, trailing in its
wake a progressive perversion of German culture. It is notable,
however, that Büchner, a contemporary of the romantics, had

1

the clairvoyance and courage to oppose health to their cult of
death; the desire to serve to their amoral aesthetic; and the
consciousness of a human "becoming" to their nostalgia for a
lost paradise (which they situated in an idealized version of the
Middle Ages). And so he takes a place in the healthy current,
which, though in the minority, continued from Heine to
Thomas Mann by way of Gottfried Keller and which preserved,
through the wanderings of modern Germany, the most precious
part of the German genius.

It is in this double perspective, very summarily outlined, that
the expressionistic adventure, from which Brecht can not be
isolated, must be situated. It is the adventure of his whole
generation, of that generation which had to face the war as
it was emerging from adolescence and then the sudden collapse
of a society whose unyielding framework could not accommo-
date such violent conflicts. Economic crises, moral confusion,
the bloody shock of conflicting classes, and the predominance
of basic needs like food, lodging, and sex are the themes leading
to a return to the law of the jungle, where the simple will to
survive demands ruse and brutality beyond compare. It is a
day-to-day battle in which millions of individuals find themselves trampled, engulfed, or deprived of orientation.

At the outbreak of the war, Brecht was twenty years old.
He was the son of a Protestant, middle-class family of Augsburg,
where his father directed a paper factory. He took some courses
in medicine in order to be mobilized immediately into a hospital
unit behind the lines. He composed songs of revolt for the
wounded men in his care. Guitar in hand, he appeared in the
avant-garde cabarets. Now the avant-garde, at this time, called
itself expressionist. What does this term mean?

The expressionists are unanimous in condemning a social
mechanism which reduces individuals to their function and
imposes upon them moral shackles whose hypocrisy had just
been demonstrated by the war. This protest would be legitimate
were it not paradoxically dependent upon a very doubtful
mysticism based on the life force. It sets up subjective intuition,

or more precisely the sexual instinct, in opposition to reason, to technology and, finally, to all culture.

In an expressionist manifesto, Kurt Pinthus writes: "People realized that a 'humanity' which depended entirely upon its works, on its technology, its statistics, its commerce, its industry and its petrified social order was becoming impossible. The attempt was made to save or reawaken the human element in man." But what exactly is this man (abstract) that is opposed to his reason and his work? Frank Wedekind, the most powerful and gifted of the expressionists (who inspired Brecht in his first years as a writer), gives us this answer in his play *The Spirit of the Earth*:

What do you see in comedies, tragedies?
Domestic animals with irreproachable feelings,
nourishing their desires on a pale, vegetarian diet
and permitting themselves only pleasant cocktail chatter. And
    just like you,
down there in the pit, one such hero can't stand
brandy and another doesn't really know if he's in love.
And there's a third despairing of the world.
For five acts he complains and no one
can make up his mind to end it all. But the real animal,
the magnificent and savage animal,
that one, ladies, you'll find him only in my plays!

Now that is reducing man to the common denominator of his bestiality. History becomes a biological process, a succinct dialectic of two terms: the vital instincts and rational institutions. You can quickly imagine the role that the proletariat will play in this. It will give rise to the revolt of the instincts, good or bad, of brute humanity against the mechanization of modern life. In revolution, the expressionists see only a stimulant to their formal dismemberment of society. Their plan? Liberate the most basic psyche, dissolve the ego (and its moral responsibilities) in the *Volk*, the people envisaged as a mystic entity. In all this, they either don't realize or choose to ignore the divisions of the technological society. This mystification leads a person like Felix Emmel to preach a "theater of worship" where an elementary communion of the masses would be established in the "pathos of the blood."

The expressionists are, evidently, the distant heirs of German romanticism. They conclude that the intellect must fail when faced with an irrational outburst of murder and oppression. And this erroneous conclusion leads them to take opposite paths, both equally pernicious. Some choose the Nietzschean exaltation of the instinct to power; the others prefer a withdrawal into the microcosm of subjectivity. The latter would invite man to change himself instead of the world. They affirm the goodness of man or rather that he ought to be good without answering the question: "How can he be good?"

But when the failure of the revolution had plunged Germany into stagnation, when the dream of a magic metamorphosis of the capitalistic society had fallen apart, when the terrible hour of disillusionment had arrived, some by their resignation, others by their active complicity, contributed to the rise of barbaric Hitlerism.

Now we must show how Brecht came to criticize and surmount this current. For, if the young Brecht was patterned at first in the expressionist mold, he almost immediately broke away from it. It is in the light of this dialectical relationship that we shall examine his first works, making an effort to separate, as he himself invites us to, "the old from the new."

2 · To Live Here

Baal · Drums in the Night · In the Cities' Jungle

BRECHT WROTE *Baal*, his first play, in 1918. In this play he set out to parody an expressionist drama by Hans Johst, *The Loner*. This work, which depicted the downfall of a poet, preached a heroism based on the will to power. Brecht followed its themes and its division into short contrasting scenes in which the influence of *Wozzeck* by Büchner is recognizable.

The violence and cynicism of Baal would not take us in (as, in a sense, they seduced Brecht) if they did not betray a need for an intense and constant exchange with the world, even though the need is, if you like, negative and perverted. Baal dreams of a fusion with the elementary forces, of a return to the vegetable life. It is the German temptation of the forest "where the light of heaven is forgotten." It is expressed by a symbolism of decomposition whose inventory has been taken by Herbert Luthy.[1] This nauseous lyricism is accompanied, however, by a fresher imagery, that of the rivers in which Baal is forever immersing himself, of the meadows, and of the winds. Now, whether it is a question of decay or of passive flow without effort, Brecht always expresses the same nostalgia for the sleep of the unconscious. This harmony between tree and earth or wind, making a better death possible, is pursued by Baal through all the forms of drunkenness: that of wine, of inter-

1 "Of Poor Bert Brecht," *Encounter*, XXXIV, July 1956, pp. 33–53.

course, and even of murder. He drinks to protest or to exalt himself or to drown his conscience—that poisoned seed. As for his sexual irritations, they have only one purpose and that is to show man in his primitive, naked state, stripped of all his ornaments, alibis, and justifications. *Man muss das Tier heraus-locken,* push the beast out into the open!

Baal is in heat: Baal wants a woman, "no matter which one, but one with a face like that of a woman." But if he is always pursuing the same face, it is because of an absence of faces. He destroys his victims and snuffs out in them whatever they possess that is irreplaceable.

SOPHIE: Do you at least know my name? I am called Sophie Barger.
BAAL: You must forget that. (*He kisses her*) Now you belong to the wind.

Now, by doing this, Baal prevents the sort of communication he was desperately searching for, the sort of communication that can be established only on the level of language, which is ruled out here. There is no human exchange between animals. There is only murder, and the love affairs of Baal end in murder.

I do not know if this self-criticism is as logical as Brecht would like, much later, to pretend. It is born, at that particular time, from an obscure uneasiness. One would say that Brecht confusedly foresees that his heroic rejection of all society is doomed to come to an impasse. Bitter irony marks Baal's end. He breaks down alone, calling in vain for the human presence he had so proudly pushed aside.

BAAL: It must be light out. I want to go outside. (*He cries out*) I am no rat. I want to go out. To get to the door!

Indeed, to go out, get out of the abyss which separates the young, bourgeois Brecht from a chaotic and extremely divided society. Rejected in his solitude and his fragility, the Brechtian man (or rather the pre-Brechtian man) gets a feeling of profound insecurity. He does just the opposite of what he wants to do. His actions get out of control and turn against him. He sees himself invested with destructive energy (living is already death), and the most intimate parts of himself remain foreign to him. Like the Mazeppa, whose unbridled career Brecht records, he is bound to the horse of his instinct and is stealthily watched by the vultures.

One notices that, from the beginning, Brecht renounces—and this is what separates him from the expressionists—all metaphysical alibis. His hope is founded on despair. He imprisons man in the world here below and delivers him over to his fellows. Then too, there is a spontaneously dialectical intuition which links decay to existence and makes an effort to convert destruction into productive energy. We can define this intuition, as does Herbert Luthy, as a "piety without transcendence," stoical and objective.

The young Brecht's hesitation is reflected in the contradictory relationships between himself and his heroes. He is not writing *Baal* to propose an ideal way of life for us, but rather to follow an experience through to its absurd conclusion. And if he is fascinated by the insolent vitality of the character, it is not without reserve. Twenty years later we are to come across Baal again under the guise of Puntila, the earthy landlord, drunkard, seducer, and a crafty, none too honest, businessman as well. But at that time Brecht will denounce him as a social curse. He will no longer be duped by the dangerous exaltation nor by his visions of a self-destruction which in the end turn against those that destiny (or rather the economy) delivers over to it. The author's criticism—founded on everyday experience with the working classes—will come from the chauffeur, Matti. But, for the time being, Brecht will paint a completely romantic picture of the people. His "workers" come, in fact, from what Marx called the *Lumpenproletariat*, the tattered proletariat. Instinctively, Brecht seeks out their company, or at least their approval. But if they admire his intelligence and courage, they would like to see these qualities applied to "something useful". The problem of an *engagement* is then hinted at in *Baal*. And, curiously enough, it remains charged with a religious significance, the words of the minister joining those of the longshoremen.

In short then, if the first draft of a social criticism is to be

found in *Baal*, it remains equivocal, abstract, and entirely in-
stinctive. "My political experience," admitted Brecht in 1939,
"was shamefully limited; but I was, nevertheless, conscious of a
great difference which divided men in their social lives, and I
did not believe that it was my duty to resolve formally the
dissonance and antagonism that I profoundly felt."

This absence of method limits the answer Brecht was to propose, two years later, to the revolutionary activities destroying
his country. Actually, in *Drums in the Night* (1920) he attacks
a real historical situation. Its context is the resignation of in-
surgent soldiers, "a symptom"—according to Rosa Luxemburg—
"of the general immaturity of the German revolution." From this
collapse, Brecht himself, who was a member of the revolutionary
council of Augsburg, gained bitter experience. How is he going
to go about expressing this experience?

The plot of the play is not original: it can be found in several
contemporary dramas. Andreas Kragler, a soldier believed to be
dead, returns to Berlin after a long captivity. His fiancée has
been promised to another, a worker who profited from the war.
Anna's parents, not caring a bit for poor Kragler, hasten the
engagement. During a supper which has been disturbed by up-
risings beginning in the streets, Anna is suddenly struck by her
love for Kragler. But while she is wandering about looking for
him, he has got mixed up with a group of workers in a tavern.
He has had something to drink; and, becoming suddenly exalted,
he leads the workers toward the district where the battles are
raging. Then he meets Anna, and after a dramatic debate, he
betrays the cause saying: "Should my meat be left to rot in the
garbage so that your ideas can go to heaven? No, but you're
drunk, aren't you? I'm a pig and the pig is going home to bed."

One could easily wonder whether Brecht, at the time, ap-
proved of this cynical choice or not. It is more likely that he
simply wanted to describe and perhaps even to explain a situation. But if he acquits his proletariat, he judges the bourgeoisie
harshly. The latter condemns itself since it cannot successfully
raise itself, in spite of all its furious patriotism, above its limited
vision and immediate interests. It doesn't even evaluate the

dangers it is facing. Soon its optimism will cause its collapse; its idealism is fatal.

Idealism? Let us make sure we understand each other. Anna's parents have a penchant for invoking, on any and every occasion, God and his celestial legions. Depending on the circumstances, they will curse Him no less naturally. Mr. Balicke, when he speaks of death (in this case, that of the artilleryman), affects the brutal language of a technician or a businessman. But this in no way prevents him from deploring the lack of an ideal in the masses: "And the worst thing, let me tell you, is the soldiers at the front. Tattered, depraved adventurers who have lost their taste for work and for whom nothing is any longer sacred, that's all they are." In fact, the bourgeois idealism is good for the others: it is a weapon for the strong and a poison for the weak. It is a meaningless word which only serves to disguise the brutality of a system where the deepest and truest sentiments are turned to derision.

Thus, the cynicism of Anna's father is fully justified; and when, short of arguments, he asks Kragler if he has the means to support his daughter, he is only verbalizing reasons of which the heart is unaware, for the moral of the system is founded precisely upon this question of means: whoever doesn't have money is a sinner, as Brecht demonstrates with frightening logic in *Mahagonny*. So he is going to grapple with a radical "demystification" of effective language or, according to him, lie. Lukacs, it is true, reproached the overformal aspect of Brecht's criticism of "theatrical cookery." When, at the end of his play, Brecht scolds the public and destroys the fiction he himself had created, when he cries out: "That was just ordinary theater. Nothing but planks and a cardboard moon. But the slaughterhouses in back are very real," he scarcely goes further than the irony that the German romantics of the time were using. What distinguishes him from them, however, is the will to overcome the alienation of poetry from the objective world. As in *Baal*, he shows man the way back to his needs. These needs, as elementary as they appear, have a moral significance. The future of man depends on their satisfaction, and their scope is wider than the limited realm of private life. Kragler's adventure is more than an accident: it poses one of civilization's problems. One of the play's characters states it with precision: "That's what's human. It concerns all of us. Just the same, he must find his wife!" But the system—which is not human—forbids the satisfaction of this just need. Anna and Kragler are under pressure from their environment; it constrains them to do harm to the most human and precious part of themselves.

ANNA: I was afraid. With my fear, I should have waited for you, but I am bad. Let go of me; everything is bad in me.

Here are the beginnings of the theme *not-want-to-but-ought-to*, which is so Brechtian. Anna's betrayal corresponds as well to that of Kragler, an honest, weak proletarian, at the mercy of people worse than himself. We shall not go so far as to say that he is the blind, unconscious toy of destiny. He is not allowed the innocence of Wozzeck. He has tendencies to see clearly, which are the beginnings of a class conscience. And yet it will be enough that an immediate, although illusory, solution is offered him for him to take refuge in it. Henceforth, he will only be able to excuse his cowardice by the "faults" of others. He will even come around to taking up the arguments of his worst enemy, Anna's bourgeois father: "They tear up newspapers in the gutters, shout down the machine guns, and think they are building a new world."

I doubt that these words reflect Brecht's opinion. They express, at best, a defiance with regard to revolutionary romanticism. If we are tempted to see the "moral" of the play in them, it is because it is still drawn from traditional theater which pretends to be impartial. It is only later that Brecht will raise the question of impartiality again, at the cost, in truth, of a political education. But for the time being, he is deceived and troubled by the failure, or rather decay, of the revolution. Just like his hero, he takes refuge (for a while) in the sphere of private interests. *Bargan Doesn't Care*, a novella published in 1921, marks a definite retreat. There Brecht turns his back on the troubling questions of the day to describe, and not without affectation, a case of sexual psychopathology. This is the curious story of a freebooter who sells out his goods, his companions, and finally himself for the love of his adversary. And he does that, explains Brecht, "simply because he was looking for something to which he could be of use."

Brecht takes up this disconcerting theme again in a play which is as untheatrical as possible, *In the Cities' Jungle* (1922). His intentions would remain obscure if he himself had not helped us, some thirty years later, in deciphering them. Let us reread the prologue: "It's Chicago, 1912. You are watching the inexplicable battle between two men. Don't trouble yourself about the motives behind this conflict. Rather get interested in the human stakes, judge with impartiality the methods of the combatants, and focus your attention on the finish." Actually, this metaphysical combat between the gangster Shlink and the honest employee Garga is absurd. Shlink wants to escape necessities (appetites to be satisfied) in order to reach an absolute and gratuitous liberty. The more futile the stakes, the more disinterested the battle. He must, then, find an adversary willing to risk everything—his job, his fiancée, the material well-being of his family—for nothing more than the pleasure of resisting him. Now, the librarian Garga would actually prefer to lose his shirt and his skin rather than sell out his insignificant opinion on an insignificant book. His frantic idealism is at least equal to that of Shlink, and their reciprocal hatred mixed with a strange love will involve them in a furious melee which will ruin them both. Garga will try in vain to escape from this hell. Sometimes, he will dream in a very middle-class way of establishing a family; sometimes, he will give in to the temptation to flee like Rimbaud, which is only, of course, a substitute for the other. But Shlink keeps inflicting the most ignominious humiliations on him. He wants to know just how far a man can go in the realm of evil and to probe the ultimate limits of his liberty. But Shlink discovers this liberty to be unbearable, "the possibilities open to man being too numerous." So unbearable is this liberty that, to escape his indetermination, Shlink makes up his mind to choose despair as a solution, to die and eliminate his conscience. The "finish" lets us in on the secret of this mania for self-destruction (which, in passing, cannot be satisfied except at the cost of the destruction of many beings):

GARGA: Language is not enough to understand each other with.
SHLINK: I've observed animals. Love, the heat of the body, is our only grace in the shadows. But it is only a union of organs; it would not be able to surmount the division caused by language. If you load a boat to the bursting point with human bodies, there will be such solitude inside that they will break down from the coldness of it. Do you hear me, Garga? Yes, solitude is so great that there is not even any more conflict. The jungle, that's where humanity comes from.

The conclusion hits hard. Deprived of his adversary, who simply declares a forfeit, Shlink takes poison. As for Garga, who inherits his goods, he goes off to look for adventure in New York, abandoning his family: "It's good to be alone."

This so ruinous metaphysical quest ends then quite flatly in lower-middle-class resignation. The Rimbaud-like adventure which seems to have had such an immense attraction for Brecht makes an abrupt turn. At the detour society waits for just the one who wanted to turn his back on it. And that is why one discovers in this "finish" Brecht's involuntary self-criticism. But let him explain it himself: "In this play I intended to study the instinct of combativeness, pure and for its own sake. But I very quickly perceived that it is difficult to depict a significant combat, and I meant by that a conflict that could prove something. My characters waged war on the family, the business of their adversary. They would go so far as to wager its 'goods' (by doing this, I was getting close, without knowing it, to the real battle which was raging around me, namely that of the classes), but they did not really succeed in reaching their adversary. My experience suddenly appeared to be more than obscure. I didn't know that, in the late phases of capitalism, the combative instinct is no more than a savage, degenerated form of sporting competition. The dialectic of my play is, by nature, purely idealistic." [2]

2 *Upon Examining My First Plays, Stücke,* Vol. 1.

It may be objected that any work of art, whether it wants to be or not, is an abstract of reality. But, like so many of his contemporaries, young Brecht got caught up in a vicious circle in pursuing an abstraction for its own sake, without reference to the real contradictions of his own time. And wanting to seize upon the essence of combat, he only demonstrated, by means of the absurd, the vanity of such an undertaking. He threw himself up against the fundamental contradiction of the capitalistic system. Namely that in promoting a production of an increasingly collective character, it only increased the isolation of individuals. The exchange of objects, founded on violence, is no longer the sign or vehicle of human exchange. In short, man alienates himself in the objects he conquers. Meeting is no longer possible unless on the plane of murder or sexuality.

Just the same, it is noticeable that this pulverization of society causes in Brecht a reflex of hatred against whoever adapts himself to it. It is the positive aspect of his revolt that always tends toward anarchy. His heroes, seeing themselves caught in the gears, sold like merchandise, throw themselves into an act of absolute protest against all forms of society. They oppose an absolute liberty to an absolute necessity. This nihilism can be easily transformed—Garga proves it—into resigned quietism. When Brecht stops isolating himself from "all these other people, all these good people, all these other worthy people at their work benches who earn their living and set good tables for all these eaters-of-bread, all these other setters-of-good-tables and good eaters-of-bread with all their good families that are so numerous—that already make a mountain—and no one spits in their soup and no one sends them off to the good beyond with a good swift kick," when he rejects without nuance all social systems of production and consumption, Brecht comes close to the mysticism which will give birth to very concrete Nazism. The fact that Brecht knew the elation of it only gives more weight to the straightening out that was to follow.

3 · The Destiny of Man Is Man
Edward II · A Man's a Man

AROUND 1923 the German theater was at an impasse. On all sides people were asking about its social function. The critic, Epstein, setting himself up as the interpreter of Max Reinhardt, was of the opinion, for example, that the classic repertory could no longer interest the spectators of a democratic era. The abortive revolution of 1918 had not succeeded, however, in really modifying the economic organization of the German stage. This failure, coupled with the political inexperience of the post-war playwrights, considerably limited any attempt at renovation. They were reduced to purely formal experiments, assuring an excessive preponderance of inventions in staging. They believed, for instance, that they were bringing Schiller up to date by decking his heroes out in bowlers and proletarian caps.

At this time Brecht was entrusted with an unimportant job as stage manager in a pocket theater in Munich. There he produced a play by Marlowe, *Edward II*. This was the first of a series of adaptations that he would borrow from the international repertory with assurance and ever growing liberty throughout his career. Brecht, who was assured of the collaboration of an already famous writer, Lion Feuchtwanger, intended to pose once again the problem, not only of the form, but even of the content of the traditional theater. What, then, can he learn from a Marlowe?

Many things which were to help him in years to come go

into his conception of an "epic theater." With Marlowe the drama remains "out in the open." It is only a slice of life and not an autonomous, closed universe where death has the last word. In reality, life never has any conclusion. Hence, we have a juxtaposition of sketches where the dramatic tension can very easily slacken and then regain force. This is the contrary of the continuous progression so dear to the French neoclassics (and, consequently, to the German neoclassics too). The Elizabethan drama, on the other hand, awakens the political sense of the spectator. The noblemen and kings who betray their country for their private interests are judged very harshly, and *by the events themselves*. This interest in teaching is translated into theater by an alternating series of action and commentary (monologues). There, characters do not submit absolutely to their destiny. That is, they strive to understand it and improve upon it and, in this way, enjoy (along with the spectator) a relative freedom.

This demonstrative conception of the theater is corroborated by a rhetoric from which Brecht will be able to profit. It will help him surmount the crisis of German verse, which was tending, at this time, to degenerate into a purely subjective musicality (Rilke). Elizabethan verse is, on the contrary, rough and gnarled but solidly constructed, with clearly marked antinomies and manners of speech. In Marlowe's work, it had not yet reached the magic richness of Shakespearian verse (which so greatly influenced German romantic poetry). Marlowe makes an effort to master a new content, with the thing to be said taking precedence over the method of saying it. The poems of Brecht in the years to come owe their tone to him. The power behind them is logical syntax instead of the irrational linkage of images. Brecht substitutes a communicative lyricism for the dreamlike discharge of the expressionists.

We may notice that Marlowe constantly refers to feudal values. If he condemns the unbounded ambition of Edward II or his peers, it is in the name of an immutable, religious order, founded on oaths, in which everyone ought to perform his function lest the equilibrium or "health" of the nation be upset.

In this medieval perspective, Marlowe outlines a certain number of political "sins": when the king betrays the people, when the nobles betray the king, or when the commoners try to rise above their station in life. In a more general way of speaking, anything is a "sin" if the private interests involved are prejudicial to the interests of the community.

In Marlowe's time, however, the ideological structure was being menaced by Renaissance individualism. A new dynamism was trying to cut a path into his work. Liberty's confused call, unable to find an objective social answer, manifested itself, in a paradoxical way, by a turning inward or refusal to act. From the Middle Ages Marlowe borrowed the symbol of the wheel of fortune upon which one ascends only to fall from a greater height. He denounces the vanity of all participation in history (which is always dependent upon destiny). This supports an argument in favor of a contemplative life, which alone can insure the tranquility of the soul. He proclaims the dignity of the victim and his victory over the hangman in the name of a moral conscience which Marlowe defines as a capacity for suffering, repenting, and pardoning. So, the liberty that he proposes is purely interior even though his sympathy (if not his reason) would go out to the individualistic, unbridled heroes.

Brecht accommodates rather badly to this contradiction. He senses, however, that it is not up to him to resolve it, and that is why he accentuates it. And this, doubtless, is the cause for this curious allusion to original sin which he devises as a sort of conclusion:

> May God pardon them at this time
> So that our generation will not have to atone for their sins.
> As for us, may he will that we
> Be not rotten
> Upon leaving the wombs of our mothers.

This is not the only place where Brecht reworks Marlowe. Having finally found the "significant" conflict that he vainly sought in *In the Cities' Jungle*, he polarizes around a restricted number of persons the social dynamisms which confront them. Had he adapted this drama ten years later, Brecht would, I

believe, have modified the light which Marlowe throws on
Gaveston, the favorite of the king. He would have made him
only the pretext (and not the cause) of the conflict of interests
in *Edward II* which opposes a royalty in search of absolutism
to a nobility attached to its feudal privileges. But at the time he
had only an inkling of these real stakes. And so it is in his
version that the assassination of Edward by Mortimer is no
longer interpreted as a passion-filled act of vengeance but as a
political action. Henceforth, the play no longer illustrates the
battle between two "temperaments," but rather allows for
the comparison of two contrary methods of combat. We have,
on the one hand, the king, the heir (like Baal and Shlink) to
the old irrational world and slave to his instincts to such an
extent that they destroy him and, on the other, Mortimer, the
cold calculator and prototype of the modern statesman. Unfortunately, Mortimer works unceasingly to conduct a rational
set of politics within an irrational system. He is caught up in the
machinery of violence as a consequence of this; this is the
fatality of power which those who make history pass on to
each other like lepers.

> Like a red and tottering moon,
> Reason
> Deserts the brain. Then
> In the nude appears
> The beast that lurks in man.

Evidently, Brecht is always distrustful of man. From him
Brecht expects the worst betrayals. If *Edward II* is compared to
Baal, we notice, nevertheless, that this theme of treason tends
to lose its metaphysical bearings. The valet Baldock betrays the
king because he has an aged mother to feed and because he must
kill to live. In shaping this character, Brecht personifies the
popular masses that Marlowe only suggests. In certain street
scenes he presents their revolt against the negligence of the
great for which they pay dearly when all is said and done. The
revolt is ineffective because it is attached to the illusory hope
that the masses will be able to profit in some way from the

quarrel between the powerful leaders. Their lack of awareness foreshadows that of *Mother Courage*.

In a word, Brecht brings Marlowe's play up to date. He modernizes it by putting a distance between it and us. In so doing, he outlines from instinct the method for his future adaptations. Our attitude toward the classics differs, in fact, from that of their contemporaries. Their works posed questions (for example, that of liberty) which history, in the meantime, has taken upon itself to answer. We know these answers and ought to take them into consideration. So it is necessary, according to Brecht, to project the works of the past and clarify their conflicts in the light of our modern conscience.

At any rate, allusions to the present are not lacking in *Edward II*. Ten years before the eruption of Nazism, Brecht, in this play, announced the concentrationary mechanism. Nevertheless, one of his characters asserts that "injustice never gets old, but justice persists." This statement betrays a belief that history is infallible and that, in the end, it always eliminates whatever there is in history which is opposed to human development. In the play, it is a question of irrational confidence in which I perceive the germ of Brechtian optimism which we shall see as a hope based on despair.

It is, however, only the germ. *A Man's a Man*, which Brecht wrote a year later, betrays his uneasiness about the "depersonalization" of the masses in the capitalistic system. This system demands such a division and specialization of work that the workers become interchangeable and completely at the mercy of the hazards of supply and demand. Henceforth, one man will be as good as another. He transforms himself to survive and forces himself to fill better the changing needs of the system. In a word, he becomes "functionalized."

Brecht attempts to demonstrate this process by means of a parable whose rather abstract and mechanical character does not exclude, however, a certain psychological accuracy. Its setting is India at the time of the British "pacification" that Rudyard Kipling (here parodied by Brecht) extolled with naïve dynamism. The dockworker Galy Gay is a man who "can't say no." His principle or driving force is not to cause any scandal, even though he is quite vain. It is enough for someone to pretend to take him seriously for him—a weakling among weaklings—actually to believe that he is strong and evil. Unfortunately, such little people believe they know everything and are never astonished by anything. For, in agreeing to don the uniform of the soldier Jip, accused of looting ("once does not form a habit"), Galy Gay lets himself get caught up in a chain of events from which he will emerge scarcely recognizable. His companions have got him involved in an illegal traffic, and then they bring quick legal action against him. He no longer dares to be either Jip or Gay (for each is liable to be executed) and he no longer even knows who he is (for he is no longer anyone). So there he is with no other choice but to become what they want him to be: a docile, anonymous, sanguine man. A sham execution illustrates this metamorphosis, and our "new man" has to give his own funeral oration.

"Was he a good man or bad?"
"Oh, he was a dangerous man."

Dangerous for whom? For the "system" which can survive only at the price of alienating the Galy Gays, so numerous a group before the advent of Hitler. We get the feeling that Brecht fears and welcomes, at the same time, this alienation. His reason approves of it, but a more intimate demand makes him protest against it. We are going to try to analyze this contradiction. In a radio commentary on A Man's a Man (1927) Brecht announces the germination of a new humanism through which man, far from letting himself be molded by the system, will transform it. Now, Galy Gay would carry precisely the seeds of this new humanism. His opportunism would allow him to adapt himself to all situations. "He seems accustomed," writes Brecht, "to putting up with many things. Only rarely does he allow himself a personal opinion. I think you are in the habit of considering a man weak who does not know how to say no. But this Galy Gay is not at all weak. Very much to the contrary, he is among the strongest of men on the condition that he can give up his private self. Galy Gay only becomes strong as a part of the masses."

Brecht, then, intends to underline certain positive aspects of the capitalistic system, which he considers to be transitory. This system, in depriving man of his individualistic pretentions, makes him recognize his true standard which is collective. This is the sense in which Marx asserts that the "personality" will blossom not in a heroic opposition to the masses, but in harmony with them. In demanding that individuals know how to adapt themselves to the changing needs of production, the industrial machine tends, to a certain extent, to "defunctionize" men. It does this by breaking down the barriers that it had imposed until that time, and, by so doing, it digs its own grave, so to speak.

These are rather hasty summaries. The "collective" actually could not have an absolute value. It is hard to see how Galy Gay's adherence to organized murder and looting could found a new humanism. In fact, he is only the dupe of this illusory agreement that the middle class proposes, denying and drowning in blood the conflict between classes.

Brecht, although he has as yet hardly touched on Marxism, senses, in a completely intuitive manner, whatever is lacking in his demonstration. The result of this is the fundamental insecurity from which most of his characters are suffering. They profane and mutilate themselves because the system wants from them only that part (not individual or private) that it can make use of. Whoever remains true to himself, assuming all the parts of himself, excludes himself from the system. The alternative makes people into their own enemies; they must make themselves the accomplices of just what is oppressing them. So we have a Galy Gay. He repudiates himself just as he has disowned his wife and his past. Distrusting himself ("I used to see my image in the water/And I know that you can die from looking at yourself that way"), rejecting the unbearable duality of his nature ("I am perhaps the double-me which has just been born/On the changing surface of the earth"), deprived of retreats in an extremely fluctuating world, Galy Gay sets himself up amidst his alienation.

> If the train does not stop, and if everyone is asleep,
> then I too want to go to bed and sleep
> my fill until the time when it stops.

We know today that the reawakening will be brutal. But Brecht, on the contrary, is a man who does not go to sleep. Painfully, he looks around for some orientation. The purposely pedantic discourse which he puts in the mouth of a soldier attributes the crisis in the modern conscience to technical progress (assembly line) and to the discoveries of science (Copernicus). Each has deprived man of his privileged, quasi-sacred place at the center of the universe. If everything is relative to everything else, we are no longer the measure for all things, which is just the same as saying that we are no longer anything. The consequences? They can be found set forth in the "Song of Things Which Pass" that the Widow Begbick chants throughout the metamorphosis of Galy Gay. Let us examine it more closely: it sheds light on the ultimate evolution of Brecht. Never does its lyricism become as melancholy, as intimate, as when Brecht is picturing the flow of history. These are the exceptional moments. Brecht then overflows into the social sphere where he intends to isolate himself.

> You can look for a long time at the nonchalant river
> which passes; it is never the same water that you are seeing,
> And never does that which flows away go back to its source.

It is Heraclitus's image; but while he was able to draw a confident force from it, a call to liberty, Brecht, on the contrary, betrays a resignation and profound anguish before the necessity of choice in an inscrutable and changing world. Our actions surpass us, and then turn against us, to such an extent that the least error can become fatal. And when we say error, we are positing a truth. But how could permanent ethic impose itself upon changing history? If there is a human permanence, it is, at best, that of my elementary needs. *I am my hunger*. Like Galy Gay, I base my choice solely upon the instinct of preserva-

tion, and I am no more than that part of myself which does not
want to die.

I have spent seven years in the same place with the same roof
Above my head.
And I was not alone.
But the one who was providing for me, a man without equal,
One fine day
I saw him stretched out, unrecognizable, under the covering of
    the dead.
And yet, that evening like the others,
I ate my dinner.
And soon I rented out to others the room where we
Used to make love.
And the room provided for me.
And now that it doesn't provide for me any longer
I eat just the same.

This is the dissociation, the desacralization of the couple in
a system in which no one can count on anyone else. This
desacralization (here I am using religious vocabulary intentionally) affects, still more profoundly, the conscience of the
Brechtian man, breaking into his feeling of identity.

> . . . I had lost my name.
> Don't tire yourself spelling your name. What for?
> Since it never serves except to name another one of them.
> Why shout your opinion so loudly? Forget it, I say.
> What were you saying a minute ago? Don't try to remember
> Something longer than it lasts.

To what does my identity adhere? To my place and function
in society. To the *name* that others give me; that is to say, to
the image that they have of me. To my goods as well. My roof,
my milk pail, the objects familiar to me—the faithful retreats of
habit—those are the things that give me the illusion of always
remaining true to myself. Anything could deprive me of them,
and then "I have lost my name." If the human manifests
itself (as Brecht will later say) in change, then my relationships
to myself and to the world are founded on uncertainty. Even
my memory is questionable. I am "a being without a navel,
floating like a bat in the night."

How is it possible not to discover here a secret nostalgia for the sacral notion of a person who goes to pieces today? For the Christian, whoever has a name (is baptized) escapes history and change. This is man's indestructible core, "the image of God." We now perceive the sense of these parodies on Biblical language to which Brecht has recourse whenever he wants to express what the philosophers have called the death of God. It is accompanied in Brecht's work by a fundamental distrust with regard to the *Word*.

> I have spoken to many people, I have heard
> Many opinions of all sorts.
> Many people were saying many things:
> It was sure and certain.
> But retracing their steps, they changed their minds.
> And about this new opinion they also said: it is certain.
> Then I said to myself: Of all the certain things
> The most certain is doubt.

Here Brecht repudiates, in an almost metaphysical way, and even in principle, objective knowledge. Doubt is established as an absolute paralysis. But at the exact instant when the contradiction attains a degree of extreme tension, a solution appears which is really only suggested. An unexpected truth emerges from the conflict between two uncertainties. It is of a dialectical nature and surpasses the limits of individual conscience. The criterion of action becomes collective. A relative and utilitarian morality of the class is founded: "A man is nothing; someone must call him." The individual alone cannot choose a meaning for his life. He only discovers his identity and his name if others need him. The destiny of man is man. Such is, for Brecht, the plank of salvation.

4 · The World Is Poor and Man Is Bad

The Threepenny Opera · The Threepenny Novel · Mahagonny

PRESENTED in Berlin in 1928, *The Threepenny Opera* made the reputation of Brecht and Weill overnight. They had been inspired by Gay and Pepusch's *Beggar's Opera*, whose two-hundredth anniversary was being celebrated. So it is a question of a parody of a parody, Brecht and Weill's English model being directed against Handel and the Italian-inspired opera. Through the medium of the conventional heroism of a court diversion, Gay and Pepusch satirized the nobility and the middle-class businessmen of their country. Macheath, in their "opera for beggars," appeared as the romantic hero par excellence and the defender of the oppressed. But he reveled in an immoral system (in spite of his own moralistic façade) to raise himself, by illegal methods, to a position of wealth and honor.

With good reason this satire was able to capture the attention of Brecht and Weill at a time when Handel was undergoing a real revival in Germany, as the very incarnation of the image of the national grandeur and dignity in the eyes of the entire right. Hadn't the parody always served to destroy anachronistic forms, devoid of all social significance? But while the attempts at revitalizing the opera (Hindemith, Stravinsky, Krenek, and Weill himself) had, until that time, confined themselves to purely formal innovations, Brecht and Weill made an effort to bring up the question of even the function of opera in a capitalistic society. Unfortunately, they remained too faith-

ful to their two-hundred-year-old model, updating it, of course,
but in an entirely schematic way. The *Beggar's Opera* has, as a
frame of reference, a very concrete situation and denounces the
vestiges of feudalism so curiously mixed with the signs of infant
capitalism. Since that time the forms of oppression have become
much more subtle and, therefore, more fearful. The organization of the class of thieves has, on the other hand, rationalized
its existence.

In adapting the cynical romantic pose of their predecessors
to their own cause, Brecht and Weill, far from attacking the
social conflicts of their own time, were creating a misunderstanding which had to turn, out of necessity, against their
naïvely revolutionary intentions. They intended to denounce
the hypocrisy and resignation of the lower middle class, but the
public saw in their songs only a secret complicity. They attributed to Brecht and Weill the immorality they had placed
in the mouths of their characters. "Brecht," writes Ernst Schumacher, "facilitated and even provoked this misunderstanding
because his heroes were in no way typical representatives of the
middle class. Furthermore, they recited abstract truths in an
abstract way."

This ambiguity is evident from the very first bars of *The
Threepenny Opera*. After an overture parodying Handelian
pomp, a street singer strikes up "Mackie's Song." In it he denounces, by means of brutal contrast, the duplicity of the
sharks whose murders are accomplished beneath a veneer of
elegance and respectability. The melody (whose outline was
conceived by Brecht himself) expresses the resignation of whoever gives up trying to understand and, therefore, to act. This
resignation is mixed with vulgar irony and mean joy as if Mackie,
the knife-artist, were assuming the repressed revolt of all those
"who remain in the shadows." Unfortunately, the popular
imagination responds with murder. It would not be surprising
if the Germans of the thirties saw in this attempt, in this dizzi-
ness of catastrophe, an echo of their most intimate aspirations.
In a way, Brecht lends his voice to the pre-Hitlerian demons,
but it is in order to subject them to the judgment of his con-

science. Berlin's sophisticated postwar audience was deceived. Easily assimilating Brecht's aggressiveness, they were unaware of his critical intentions and whisked away his irony.

Irony is a double-edged sword. The example of the Young Germany movement, born around the middle of the preceding century in the ruins of the romantic adventure, had already shown that irony is incapable of seizing on social conflicts in all their complexity. Stripped of realism, it is quite precisely "this absolute negation by which the subject refers back to himself in order to resolve the contradictions of the real" (Hegel). Brecht had wanted to parody the customs of the middle class through those of the thieving classes. He felt the irrational killer-like character of the system—there is much less difference between a businessman and a gangster than is commonly supposed —without understanding, however, its workings. The absence of a real and collective antithesis (the organized proletariat) to the immoral thesis of his heroes weakens his criticism. This absence limited the extent of his criticism to "abstract man," bad in himself.

To a certain extent conscious of this deficiency, Brecht expected the music to bring it all into focus. Rejecting its traditional use, he demands that, far from drowning the text in order to awaken the confused emotions of the spectator, music be separated from the text in a radical way and that it comment on or, when necessary, contradict the text. Kurt Weill: "I set up my music in opposition to the action, knowing that music excludes, by its essence, all realism." Inspired by the technical contribution of jazz, our composer then set out to combat—from the inside—the narcotic powers of music. More exactly, he made an effort to dissociate the positive and negative aspects from it. He intentionally used its vengeful dynamism (the racial protest of the American Negroes) in order to bring to light the subversive intention of Brecht's text. But in the absence of a really effective antitoxin in the action of the opera, the partition could only flatter the most equivocal tendencies of the contemporary spectator. The parody was wide of the mark: what it wanted to get rid of, it had dumped into the "stew."

And yet, in spite of these weaknesses, *The Threepenny Opera* has lost none of its freshness. The events of the last thirty years have demonstrated the deficiencies in the values upon which we had founded our human relationships. Man remains at war with man. In friendship, love, or pity he finds only a fleeting truce. He has to save his skin, and nothing is sacred to him any longer except his life. He will betray his wife, his friends, and his children. Once again Brecht confronts man with his death, and in doing this, Brecht obliges him to recognize his fundamental solitude. No longer can anything save him, not money, nor ruse, nor even the tenderness of others. The death of a man is nothing, and that is why it is so scandalous. And as always when Brecht describes death throes, a lament arises from it, a confused appeal for solidarity.

The outcome is only hinted at, and it is really contradictory. Peachum (who is, to a great extent, the incarnation of Brecht's pessimism) broods in an absolute and universal distrust. He is going to be more of a shark than the sharks. He knows that pity is capricious and quickly deadened. It is the alibi of those who cannot resolve themselves to gaze upon the misery they have caused. Like all sentiments, it can be unloosed, directed, and exploited on the condition that man and his psychological scope are well understood. And that is why Peachum rationalizes mendicancy and organizes it on a large scale. For him, man is only an instrument. In order to manage him, he will only have to hold himself aloof from the human: hence his precautions against love. He is, alas! only too right: Macheath, his competitor and the lover of his daughter, is forever stumbling on this accursed sexuality which is easily the worst of man's enemies. The little amorous interludes that he snatches from the unpitying "struggle for life" will bring about his downfall. The conventionally lyrical, and yet heartrending, words that he exchanges with Polly after her brief wedding night are based on a misunderstanding. Both agree, while playing the dupes during an instant of exhilaration, but even while they are singing their unanimity, Brecht and Weill are reminding us with cruel irony of the secret division by which all love is cursed. For Macheath will have nothing more pressing to do than to go over to the brothel at Turnbridge while his best girl will deliver him over to the police for a mouthful of bread. The "Song of Solomon" that she strikes up upon completion of her betrayal is identical, to a great extent, with the defeatism of Peachum. In it the great men of history are derided. The higher you climb, the harder you fall. It is better, then, to remain in the shadows and give up all pretentions to glory, power, knowledge, and love. There is the defeatism of little people: a distrust, prudence, and an absence of heroism and ambition which would permit them, perhaps, to have the last word. Brecht seems tempted by their limited wisdom. Witness his "Ballad of Comfort" (gobble a meal first and worry about the morality of it afterwards), where he mocks the impotence of the intellectual, thirsting for truth in a world given over to violence. But fifteen years later, Brecht will take up the same tune again to thrash the satraps of Hitler's regime who were guilty of having chosen comfort. And he himself, in spite of his cynical words, will choose to be "poor and solitary, reckless and wise."

This paradox is outlined as early as *The Threepenny Opera*. I am thinking of the end of the first act. The Peachum family— father, mother, and daughter—discuss, in the lyrical mode, the "insecurity of the human condition." Why can't man be happy or good in this short life? Because this world is so poor, so badly made, that the most spontaneous virtues—fraternity, faithfulness, compassion, and the desire for peace—turn against whoever practices them. But at the same time that Brecht seems to touch the depths of despair, a strange note comes to the surface; it is timid, grave, and unexpected and is underlined by a quasi-liturgical melody:

> When everyone is finally good, His kingdom will be near.
> Who would not rest in His light?

Images like these nourish and move the depths of the soul. From it Brecht derives the energy which will permit him to confront, with the end in mind of transforming it, a system where man can survive only if he "tortures unceasingly, loots,

attacks, slits the throat of and devours his neighbor." If he
denounces the inhumanity of this man, it is because he sees a
positive value in the notion of the human. It is, however, true
that he proposes a new definition of it. He remarks in his commentaries on *The Threepenny Opera* that friendship is true only
in the sense that it is limited. Nothing is pure in man; his
noblest instincts are contradicted by others—for example, that
of security. So let us accept him as he is, divided, desiring and
not being able, fighting ceaselessly against the world that stifles
him, a victim after all is said and done, but a magnificent
victim. It must be noted that Brecht restricts himself to history,
excluding all miracles, that is to say, any invasion of man by
forces which would surpass him and would wrench him from
his natural condition. So we have a relative moral law lacking
any means of escape into the metaphysical. Fifteen years later,
in *The Life of Galileo*, Brecht will follow to its logical conclusion this morality, founded not on grace, but on justice.

Desirous as always of correcting his mistakes, Brecht wrote, at
the beginning of his exile, a *Threepenny Novel*, which is, to
some extent, a glossary to accompany the opera. There he makes
an effort to turn his subjective uneasiness into an effective criticism, or I should say, usable criticism. He situates his characters
in a more precise context: the imperialistic era whose essence
and decline were announced at the same time by the Boer War.
Above all, he creates a new character, the soldier Fewkoombey,
thus individualizing the proletariat which, up until that time,
he had left in the shadows of anonymity. In the opera we were
witnessing the conflicts of the great, forgetting their victims. The
novel reminds us that the social stakes of the drama are to be
found elsewhere: in the exploitation of the masses by a few
people.

Truthfully, the work hardly lives up to our accustomed idea of
a novel. In it, Brecht cannot keep from anticipating the events
that he is going to describe; he renounces all effects of surprise
or illusion. He brings our attention to bear on the whys and
wherefores of things; he forbids us any romanesque communion.
And yet, the ironic intervention of the author can be traced

back to a romanesque technique that the German romantics
had instituted and that is found throughout the nineteenth
century up to the time of Thomas Mann. But Brecht redirects
its use to social ends. If he applies a "noble" language to very
commonplace events, however everyday they may be in themselves, it is because he wants to denounce the strangeness of it.
The characters, setting themselves apart from themselves, examine their objective situation. For an instant they pry themselves away from their destiny and their blindness. They inform
themselves and us about their lot. The novel, in Brecht's case,
is forever overflowing into the realm of the theater. It is impossible for him not to take part, not to point out, behind the
facts, the contradictions that they hide. Besides, objectivity does
not necessarily mean impartiality. It is, then, a question of
denouncing the law of the jungle which reigns over the economic relationships in a "liberal" society, whatever semblances
of lawfulness may veil it. The jungle is only a jungle for the
hunted; the lions know its laws from experience. Hence the
necessity arises for Brecht to enlighten the man in the street on
the mechanisms which control his life, now unchaining war or
crisis, now giving an illusory sense of being better off. These
mechanisms are so obscure that our man is tempted to take them
for an immutable fatality upon which he could not exercise the
least influence. Now, here, Brecht is writing a "novel of business,"
and the description of economic phenomena rates at least as
much space as that of feelings. The soldier Fewkoombey "had
he been instructed," "had he taken the pains to think," "had
he been able to express himself," would not be in the situation
in which he finds himself. So Brecht places his know-how (his
"culture") at the disposal of all the ignorant Fewkoombeys in
his country. He shows them that the fluctuation of prices has
nothing to do with the rain or good weather; in a word, he gives
them an insight "into the secret of the gods."

But these gods, who are they? To be precise, they are businessmen. Are they free? No, they are not, because the system from
which they profit alienates them from life too. They all live in
temporary quarters without rest, pleasure, or comforts. They

possess nothing; they operate in the abstract. They make money with the wind, playing on weakness, directing the force of others so that they will profit from it. For debts are the prime movers in business. And all that comes, according to Macheath, from the fact that today "property is no longer real property."

So there is a fundamental insecurity from which our adventurer tries to escape by resorting to a very middle-class recourse, habits. If he goes to a bawdy house every Thursday, it is not because he enjoys himself there. Very simply, he is making an effort to dam up the mysterious and inadmissible sexuality whose danger to business he is very well aware of. Nomadism, the game of chance, instability are the daily lot of the proletariat. The middle class succeeds more or less in satisfying its instinct to preservation. "Sexuality," writes Brecht, "does not give a basis for the conduct of Macheath: it contradicts it." The Macheath of the novel is not, then, like the one in the opera (and above all the one in the film), a Don Juan whose excessive vitality could conceivably captivate us. He is a sickly person in whom love is never anything more than an instrument of power.

If Macheath is a hangman of hearts, Peachum is a hangman of work. Does he really work? No, he betrays his unfathomable boredom. He steals, bit by bit, the poor money of the poor people, knowing all the time that all the money in the world cannot save him. It is a morbid passion, a mechanical activity, a taste for accumulation for its own sake, an art for art's sake. His despair is such that he accomplishes everything with the certainty of its uselessness. His distrust is so absolute that he ends by distrusting his distrust itself. But whatever the distrust of the powerful, whatever their conflicts of interest, they always have one sole prey, a single enemy: the poor. The system cannot exist without them. If one of the terms of the dialectic is missing, then the whole thing melts away. And yet we have seen that the wealth of the wealthy (which implies the poverty of the poor) is an abstract wealth, without joy. It is not the sign of any value. For Fewkoombey, who foresees that science would be able to pull him out of his misery, a half-volume of the Encyclopaedia Britannica represents an infinite value. For

Polly it is nothing, and yet she is burning with the desire to steal it from him. The value of an object, then, is entirely relative. It depends upon its usefulness. But things are in the possession of those people who know least about how to take advantage of them. It is an unjust ownership because it is sterile. The system that is founded upon it, then, is inhuman. This system aims at immutable repetition rather than at production. It goes against life: its moral is a morality of suicide.

Fewkoombey is a victim of it. He dies alone, "hanged in the presence of an applauding crowd of small merchants, dressmakers, war cripples, and beggars." However, his eyes are at least half open. He heard a beautiful sermon on the parable of the talents, which says that from him who has nothing will be taken even what little he does have. All men, states the archbishop, are equal in the beginning and the success of some is only the just recompense of their will. But a dream reveals the fraud in this sermon to our scapegoat. The enigma suddenly clears up: "The talent of man is man." In this system people succeed only by exploiting their fellow men. The dream ends with a condemnation of Christ. Meanwhile, we should be careful not to mistake Brecht's intentions. If he puts Christianity on trial here, it is not in order to reject its aspirations for more human *relationships*. What he accuses it of is metaphysically justifying man's exploitation of man. The profound sense of the parable (man ought to make use of nature) is accepted. Its social utility is rejected.

Now let us return to *Mahagonny*, written five years earlier. There, by means of violent imagery, Brecht symbolizes contemporary anarchy. He points out its existence and describes it, but he lacked the method which would permit him to analyze its real causes. The Marxists, of whom Brecht was still unaware at this time, had demonstrated that capitalistic production brings about a materialization, or an alienation (*Verdinglichung*) of all human relationships in money. "The worth of man," wrote Engels, "is a function of his *solvency*." Brecht condemns this monstrosity, but he is tempted once again to attribute to it an almost metaphysical foundation (if not justification).

Three condemned criminals decide to found a city in the
desert. It is to be called Mahagonny and will be based on
nothing except human estrangement. It is a mirage-city where
the hunted will eagerly flock because they believe in a happiness
which is not earned but stolen in an instant. Obviously, it is a
trap and, in fact, our three adventurers know that you can "pry
gold more easily away from men than from mountains." The
happiness they offer is very expensive. Based on magic, this
happiness is illegitimate.

> . . . for the voluptuousness of man
> is to suffer nothing and be capable of everything.

Brecht wants to demonstrate that the magic of money,
alcohol, and sex is, in the last analysis, illusory and destructive.
In fact, everything in the acrid, melancholy, sophisticated atmos-
phere of this play with its "songs," drugs, bars, smoke, and electric
lights, everything indicates that Brecht only uses magic in order
to denounce more effectively the magic of his times. He
demonstrates this by means of the absurd which, once again, is
not without a certain ambiguity.

But the first immigrants are already arriving in Mahagonny,
fleeing the misery and solitude of the tentacular cities. And
since they need women, a commerce starts up immediately.
The man named Paul Ackermann distinguishes himself from
his companions from the very first because he is more demanding. The face alone is not enough for him: he is the only one to
ask the *name* of the woman he is going to choose as a companion. What he is looking for is basically impracticable, and
his disillusion is in proportion to his strong desires. "All those
who really search," writes Brecht, "are disillusioned." What,
then, in the last resort, is this son of Baal looking for? He
wants an absolute liberty with which to use up his overabundant
energy. He is the most human of all of them because man is
defined by the growth of his needs and also by their satisfaction.
Now, at Mahagonny this growth is impossible. There, you are
offered "rest, harmony, whiskey, and girls" without the least
effort demanded on your part. But with the disappearance of

effort, liberty disappears too, and that is why Paul Ackermann is stifled in this world without either perspectives or conquests. His revolt breaks loose during a night of terror while a typhoon menaces the city.

In the face of this unleashing of destructive and irrational forces, the people of Mahagonny discover the fragility and the solitude of man's condition.

> Wherever you go
> it's useless;
> wherever you are
> you're caught.
> The best thing would be
> to stay seated,
> waiting for
> the end.

Ackermann rejects this resignation. He tries to construct a new morality in conformity with the laws of nature. But what laws? Any form of life must yield its place to other forms: "everything which arises from the dust will return to dust." Nothing lasts; nothing escapes the game of life and death. So you have to play the game. Since our moment of existence is so brief, since it is our only possession, since there is nothing beyond and since our condition is that of all animals, let us do as they do, let us imitate the typhoons which do as they please, for "nothing is forbidden." And so Paul Ackermann proclaims the four commandments which are to reign in the new Mahagonny: "Gorge, kiss, box, drink."

Here Brecht seems to approve the law of the strongest, a "free competition" which is ruled over by nature. The absence of certainties ("you can't trust anything") which had been, until that time, at the source of his despair suddenly appears as a motive for human liberty and excess. This dynamism is offset, unfortunately, by a gratuitous and bloodthirsty disorder. People will object that Brecht only pretends to adopt this pre-Nazi ethic so that he may better combat it and that, in his play, it ends in an impasse. This does not take into account the fact that he couches the statement of this position in the words of

Paul Ackermann, a victim of the system. Brecht makes him the symbol of the city that dies with him. In *Mahagonny* the members of the proletariat assume the defects of the system. It is they who betray their friends and the most precious parts of themselves as soon as money enters the picture. This ambiguity shows up the weakness of Brecht's demonstration.

How is he going to conclude his drama? Paul has bet, against all the rules of good sense, on his friend. He is ruined; and, in order to forget this misfortune, he drinks and buys rounds. The vanity of this escape becomes striking during a scene in which three drunkards hoist each other up onto a billiard table that they take to be a ship, believing that in this way they can flee the smoke-filled trap into which they have fallen. Now arrives the time to pay up. Paul, having sobered up, sees this law of the strongest, which he had so joyously proclaimed, turn against him. His friend and even the woman he loved (and who loved him) abandon him. A briskly conducted trial ends, for him, in the electric chair. For in this system there is no worse crime than that of not having any money. And Brecht specifies that no one in the room will be willing to use any of his possessions to come to Paul's aid however disagreeable his execution may seem. Paul's final confession is bitter. Whatever money provides is rotten, and whatever is taken by force does not even exist. Friendship, happiness, and liberty cannot be bought.

It is noticeable that Brecht "historicizes," to a certain extent, the impossibility of men counting on men. He attributes human solitude and insecurity to the rule of money, and that is progress. The end of his modern Babylon will in no way be due to some apocalyptic punishment. Turned over to the anarchical procession of demonstrators who proclaim the benefits of the "battle of all against all," Mahagonny will die of its own contradictions. And for Brecht, this battle has no end or outcome.

In 1930 this pessimism could only scandalize the Leipzig middle class, who were then appealing, all evidence to the contrary, to order and health. But a year later when the play was presented in Berlin, the battle of the classes had taken such a sharp turn that the scandal lost its edge. Then Nazism was offering an alternative to the disorder. The vulgar materialism of Brecht could only cause confusion. The least one can say is that he was not yet, by any means, convinced of the historic mission of the working classes. To what then should he attach himself henceforth?

Still, Brecht wrote (as always, with Kurt Weill) *Happy End*, which was a fiasco. In it he parodied himself, drunk with his own wine. A rupture began to become evident; besides, events began to happen at a quickened tempo. One could rightly say that after *Mahagonny* Brecht parted company with the middle classes. This decisive step is due to his study of Marxism.

5 · In the Marxist School

Lindbergh's Flight · Didactic Play for Baden-Baden on Harmony · He Who Said Yes, He Who Said No · The Measures Taken · The Mother · Saint Joan of the Stockyards · The Exception and the Rule

IMMEDIATELY FOLLOWING the war, a few young German composers founded the *Neue Musik* movement. Taking their inspiration from the innovations of form of Stravinsky and Schönberg, they nevertheless contested the social influence of their art. "Their public," a young composer wrote, "has remained the same. It is furnished with traditional opera or concert forms of music, and submits to them passively, finding in them enjoyment, relaxation, and distraction." To remedy this situation, our pioneers intended to turn music, on the contrary, to instructive ends. They founded festivals at Baden-Baden in order to try out their music with amateur musicians and actors. The active participation of the spectator should, according to them, stimulate community feeling. Thus they rejoined the tradition of the *Lehrstücke* (or didactic plays) which the German humanists of the sixteenth century had used to inculcate in their students a behavior in line with the ideals of the growing middle class. Following their example, the *Neue Musik* proposed to found new human relationships on the ruins of a decaying society.

To a certain extent, this program was in line with the preoccupations of Brecht and Weill even if the former had already posed the problem with more insight. "The great apparatuses like the opera, the theater, or the press," wrote Brecht, talking about *Mahagonny*, "impose their demands while remaining, so to speak, incognito. They only exploit the production (music, text, criticism) of the intellectual workers who participate in their gains and are, for this reason, linked to the ruling classes but remain, socially, members of the proletariat. In spite of all this, our intellectual workers stubbornly believe that all this mechanization has no other goal than showing off their production to its best advantage. This illusion has grave consequences. For, believing themselves in possession of an apparatus which in effect possesses them, they defend an apparatus which they no longer control and which is no longer, as they still believe, an instrument in the service of the producers, but an instrument directed against them, eliminating all production which does not conform to its standards. People say that a work is good and they mean (but don't say it): good for the apparatus. Now, this apparatus is determined by the social system and accepts only that which assures its place in this system."

The result is a restriction of creative liberty, to which, however, Brecht attributes a positive value. He adds: "The individual can no longer be content with *expressing himself*. He is led toward and put to the test of solving the problems of the collective character. The trouble is that, for the time being, the means of production do not yet belong to the producers and that, consequently, the work becomes merchandise and subject to the general laws of merchandise. Art is merchandise; it could not be produced without the means of production, or to put it another way, without the machinery!"

In agreeing to produce plays for the Baden-Baden festivals, Brecht knew perfectly well that it could only be a question of a laboratory experiment. He had absolutely no pretentions about modifying the official apparatuses; at the very best, he made an effort only to perfect a theatrical technique, from which the "cookery" would be eliminated to the advantage of the instructive. This word ought to be more precisely defined. Didactic plays must not be confused with "thesis" plays. The latter use a naturalist technique to "move" the spectators. The thesis is introduced, so to speak, on the sly. As for Brecht, he lays his cards on the table. His problem is not one of verisimilitude, but of communication. The spectators hold the score in their hands and intervene in their own good time. They are, of course, subject to a strict discipline (musical and verbal) which is a condition of true liberty according to Brecht.

Lindbergh's Flight (1928–1929), the first didactic play by Brecht and Weill, illustrates this principle: "doing is worth more than feeling." Written for schoolboys, it makes an effort to establish a just balance between the producer (or active spectator) and the apparatus (under the circumstances, the radio). This exercise in precision aims at eliminating all attempts at identification with the hero, this Lindbergh who had just crossed the ocean.

The trouble is that Brecht lets himself become involved in a new mythology: that of scientific progress. The discipline that he opposes to the contemporary disorder is abstract. The virtues that his hero portrays in his fight against the unchained elements are very traditional. The political evolution of Lindbergh was soon to prove their completely relative value. Brecht's appeal,

> Help us
> to combat the primitive
> to liquidate the beyond and
> to chase the gods from the places
> they pour out of

while putting the accent on the conquest of nature rather than on a transformation of society, is derived from a shortsighted cult of science. Disorder is attributed to ignorance, and God (that is to say the unknown) becomes the source of all evils. Brecht also betrays a curious timidity when he concludes:

> Around the end of the second millennium A.D.
> there arose
> our ingenuity of steel.
> It displayed possibilities
> without making us forget
> the inaccessible.

That, in his new version of the *Flight* (*Didactic Play for Baden-Baden on Harmony,* 1929), he corrected the word "inaccessible" by changing it to "not-yet-attained," underlining in a note the error he had committed, is a detail that proves that he was getting ready to go beyond the pseudo-materialism of the first years of his career. He was about to question the technique, which he had earlier eulogized, as to its goal. The naïve vanity and the conquering fervor of our aviators (whose machine has crashed) are denounced. For, in spite of their exploits,

> The price of bread has not gone down,
> But
> misery has accrued to our cities
> and for a long time no one has known
> what a man is.
> So, while you were flying, one of your fellow men
> was crawling
> on the ground, lacking everything human.

This division in the human element, which is accentuated more than resolved by technology, forces us to question the relationships of man to man. The *Didactic Play for Baden-Baden* has precisely as its object the acquisition of a new human harmony. In using the precise term *Einverständnis* (understanding, in the sense of "to have an understanding with someone"), Brecht already shows within what rational perspective this harmony is going to be placed.

The text is among the most analytical, with a quasi-linear lyricism. Its implications appear only after an effort to analyze and reflect. Brecht invites his spectators to declare themselves

> in agreement that everything ought to be changed,
> world and men,
> but above all the disorder
> of classes which results from
> exploitation, but also from ignorance.

What he is denouncing here is the inadequacy of anachronistic ethics and a new situation created by technology. The result is a false relationship between man and his work, nature, collectivity, death and, finally, the truth. The harmony formulated by Brecht depends on the fundamental question: "Do men help one another?"

Brecht answers no. In a system based on violence all aid is treacherous and self-interested. Then, it is necessary to approach "cruel reality with still more cruelty" and combat violence with violence. Brecht applies this moral to the aviators who have crashed, going so far as to refuse them a glass of water to relieve their agony. The conclusion is excessive, and a Marxist could not, I think, approve. The example is badly chosen and without social pertinence. The reason is that Brecht, for the time being, was fascinated by a personal problem. He had introduced death into his debate. In his opinion, you die alone, and the only effective aid is having the right attitude, *eine Haltung*.

> THE CHORUS: We can't do anything for you.
> It is only an attitude
> that we might be able to give you.
> Die, but learn,
> learn, but learn properly.

What attitude? A commentary sums it up in an almost liturgical tone: "If you want to overcome death, you must know it and be in accord with it." Brecht also specifies the dialectic of becoming. Life only progresses by a death, a constant negation of that which *is*. To become attached to what exists is to exclude yourself from life, refusing a productive death only to become engulfed in an isolated, sterile, absolute death. But to be in harmony with death is, on the other hand, "to enter into the river," to espouse becoming, to oppose no resistance to it. From him who is attached to nothing, nothing can be taken. Since death will force us to "make a gift of more than we possess," we must remain absolutely poor, renouncing things, ideas, and even our own existence. To put it another way, using a mystic image, we must join the greatest through the smallest part of ourselves.

That clarifies this sort of last judgment or discrimination to which the chorus subjects the aviators who have crashed. The three mechanics, after relentless interrogation, are brought around to the realization of their "smaller dimension," of their relativity. Their exploit, measured on the scale of not-yet-attained, is limited. They realize this just as they realize that no one is awaiting their return, that they are only "a few among us," that is to say, *nothing* since absolutely no one needs them. Thus, they have understood the lesson of death and, at the moment of fading away, they suddenly perceive that they are no longer alone. They overcome their solitude in the consciousness of their humility. And so we have the tribunal rescuing them from death and inviting them to transform life so that it will be in harmony with death.

Brecht's dialectic is, then, devoted to revolutionary purposes. It totally rejects conquest in order to surpass conquest. This renunciation is productive since it only abandons all values in order to establish more human ones. But the aviator Charles Nungesser, for one, did not understand the lesson of death. He believed himself to be more than his function; he didn't fly for anyone; he flew for flying's sake. In so doing, he condemned himself. For in depriving him of his airplane, of the work of others, you would deprive him of his *raison d'être*. Man's function is to be useful to others. He only exists through our need for him.

> THE CHORUS: How was he discovered?
> In giving him a job.
> In being summoned, he was created;
> In being transformed, he was given existence;
> whoever needs him, knows him
> whoever uses him, makes him grow.
> Whatever lies there without a job
> is in no way human.
> Die then, you-who-are-no-longer-a-man!

While Brecht, up until this time, had held to a primitive materialism, we now find him making an effort to solve a personal problem: "What are the necessary virtues for the man who wants to revolutionize the world?" Brecht feels a need for harmony with the masses, without succeeding, however, in establishing it in a concrete fashion. For this reason, he has recourse to traditional values. He transfers the notion of *God* to that of the *collective*. So all he has done is change absolutes.

This is where his monastic concept of the revolutionary movement comes from as well as his poorly disguised borrowings from the Christian "consensus" of the total submission to the divine will. The *Didactic Play for Baden-Baden* abounds in Biblical reminiscences.[1] They institute poverty as a cardinal virtue. To this a Marxist would answer that discipline is never an end in itself and that it results from the concrete demands of the struggle. A Christian critic would also, I believe, adopt the same attitude. A total renunciation is justified only if it is founded on the hope of a transcendence. This is what caused a Catholic journalist to denounce in Brecht "an obedience without a master, a curious confusion of Christian and pagan attitudes."

Brecht was long in realizing this ambiguity. *He Who Said Yes*, "a school opera" that he wrote the same year, is really a caricature of this abstract discipline which he had just expounded.

Brecht was inspired by a play of the fifteenth century, the *Taniko*. He was beginning to discover, at this time, the Chinese and Japanese theaters, finding in them a confirmation of his own research. In effect, the Chinese actor never confuses himself with his character. His impersonal and demonstrative attitude is directly opposed to our theater of illusion. "So," writes Brecht, "the events presented on the stage excite amazement; the everyday is wrenched away from the sphere of the natural, of evidence." This is the embryo of the famous *Verfremdungs-Effekt* to which we shall return.

The theme of the *Taniko* is precisely that of harmony, of a harmony pushed to its ultimate conclusion, since it implies suicide.

> Many say yes without being in agreement.
> From many nothing is asked and many
> agree with false things.
> It is then important to learn a real harmony.

And this is illustrated by a parable. When an epidemic breaks out, some students decide to go and seek the help of

[1] To the question, "What is the book that influenced you the most?" asked by a German magazine, Brecht answered, "You are going to laugh: the Bible!"

a foreign doctor. An urchin who wants to bring back a remedy for his sick mother joins them. After a few days of climbing, the child is all worn out. His companions decide to abandon him. However, they respect the secular custom which demands that a victim be interrogated and be in agreement with his sacrifice. The custom satisfied, they continue their journey,

> . . . deploring the sad turn of events,
> no one more guilty than his neighbor.

The dryness of the tone would lead one to believe that Brecht approves this solution. Yet it is more probable that he wrote this play with provocative intentions. And what he is provoking here is a just reaction to an unjust event. Should the life of an individual be sacrificed in favor of a collective good? The students' answer conforms typically to the custom. This custom is not even discussed. Neither by the executioners nor by the victim. It would not be astonishing if the middle-class criticism of the thirties did not question it any further either. "The child acts and thinks," writes Walter Dirks, "as if there were an imperative ethic or an appeal from God behind the actual facts of the situation which confronts him." At any rate, the play was adopted by a great number of public and religious schools. It gave rise to reservations only among the students of the Karl-Marx-Schule in Berlin with whom Brecht and Weill discussed the play. If the criticism of these young actors and spectators is analyzed, it will be perceived that they question even the custom itself and that they wind their way, not without difficulty, toward a third, revolutionary solution which, in any event, is more practical.

Taking these remarks into account, Brecht reworked his play. The second version, entitled *He Who Said No*, reexamines more or less the data of the problem, but at the moment of choice, the child rebels:

THE CHILD: Whoever says *a* is not obliged to say *b*. I wanted to look for a remedy for my mother, but now that I am sick myself, that is no longer possible. And I want to go home immediately, in conformity with this new situation. And I don't see that the old custom has anything to do with it. Rather what I need is a new custom which we are going to institute without delay: the custom which says that in each new situation one thinks it out anew.

THE STUDENTS: What this child is saying is, if not heroic, at least sensible.

> THE CHORUS: So the friends swept up their friend
> and they founded a new custom
> and a new law.
> Side by side, they walked close together
> to face the blame
> to face the laughter, their eyes tightly shut,
> no one more cowardly than his neighbor.

It is noticeable that Brecht, in his second version, avoids the problem that he had posed in the first. He no longer balances the salvation of a collectivity with that of an individual, but the health of an old woman with the life of her child. He balances them so well that what is lost on one side is gained on the other. There is no doubt that in agreeing to submit to the criticism of a revolutionary organization (the Karl-Marx-Schule), Brecht was preparing to enter into direct relations with the working movement which, until that time, he had known only in a completely bookish way. Anyway, with *The Measures Taken* he resolutely attacks certain problems that were being posed for the Communist party during the thirties.

Of all Brecht's plays, *The Measures Taken* is perhaps the one which caused the most scandal. The Marxists themselves never approached it without caution. It is possible that Brecht, like all neophytes, inclines toward an abstract extremism. He agrees, however, to situate the work in its historical context. In 1930, Germany was faced with an unheard-of crisis (six million out of work) which accelerated the growth of fascism. The dictatorship of the proletariat in one lone country only accentuated the battle of the classes, calling for violent measures on both sides. Brecht cannot be reproached for having confronted a moral problem that the Communists themselves too often tried to ignore, without softening it—that of the death penalty for political motives.

In a conversation that he had with Pierre Abraham just before his death, Brecht insisted that *The Measures Taken* was not in any way meant for the public, but only for the actors, who were to find in it an "exercise in dialectic." And it was meant to induce them "to take aim at particular points with the coolness of a billiard player." In the light of the evidence this is a retrospective interpretation, but one that can be accepted since Brecht himself enjoins us not to impose a definitive sense on his works, their dialectic being linked to that of history. In this play he depicts an imaginary episode in the Chinese revolution. Four agitators submit their illegal activities to the judgment of a *Kontrollchor,* a poetic reincarnation of the Party. Alternating the roles for the purposes of dialectic, our actors report how they were induced to liquidate a young comrade. It must be made clear that Brecht in no way presents the latter as a "rat." He is an impulsive, generous fellow of whom neither the good will nor the courage could be doubted. Because of this his execution is all the more scandalous to traditional morality. But it is just this morality, based on absolute values like justice, liberty, kindness, etc., that is being swept aside by Brecht. Taking his inspiration from Lenin, he substitutes instead a morality of combat. And this is the provisionary and relative morality of immediate decisions made in times of disorder.

THE AGITATORS: To kill inspires us with horror and
yet we kill, not only the others, but ourselves as well if need be.
For violence alone can transform
This murdering world: whoever lives
knows that.
We are not yet permitted, we used to say,
not to kill.
THE CHORUS: It is not you who have condemned your young comrade,
but reality.
THE AGITATORS: We have reflected, searching for
a better solution.
Now it's your turn to reflect; find
a better solution.

However, there can be no morality, even a relative one, without some constant criterion. Brecht dryly points out the criterion

of this morality: "Of all the virtues, he who fights for communism keeps only one: that of fighting for communism." Subjective kindness will no longer suffice: henceforth, it must be
effective. If our agitators execute their comrade, it is in no way
to punish him, but only to keep him from being harmful. This
law of the sword is applicable only to those who freely adhere
to the ultimate ends which are its basis and cause. The quasi-
monastical profession of faith of the young comrade points out,
at the same time, the ends and the instrument: "I approve the
decisions of the Communist party, which fights against exploitation and ignorance, for a classless society." As a soldier of the
revolution, he accepts a rule which can turn against him, if he
betrays it. The scene entitled "the obliteration" states the
exact implications of this engagement.

THE CHIEF OF THE CELL: From this instant forward, you are no
longer yourselves. But all of you, without names or mothers, you
are blank pages upon which the Revolution will write its directives.

Our agitators symbolize this sacrifice by donning masks.
Brecht, in a stage direction, makes it clear that this scene is by
no means a ritual. It is a question of an *Umfunkionierung*, or
change of social function. The goal of the scene is not to
"glorify" a human excess, but to make it "plausible." And so
it is necessary for the actor to put the accent on the rational
motives of irrational proceedings. The questions that the chief
poses to his comrades are chanted. They express the moral
beauty of accomplished sacrifice. But the agitators, who are
sacrificing themselves, answer each time with a prosaic "yes"
which shows how much reflection has gone into their acceptance
and how bare it is of all exaltation.

Brecht was, no doubt, thoroughly involved in the problem
while writing *The Measures Taken*. Marxist criticism of the
thirties, however, received it with reserve. They contested the
tactical principles which Brecht attributed to the Communist
party. Thus, when Brecht writes

> He who fights for communism
> must know how to fight or refuse battle,

speak the truth or not speak it,
render service and refuse his services,
keep his promises and not keep them,
expose himself to danger and flee danger,
gain recognition and remain invisible.

he certainly paraphrases one of Lenin's sentences (so often quoted by the forces of reaction), but while the latter derives a rule of action from a concrete situation (the setting up of cells in the trade unions of prerevolutionary Russia), Brecht establishes it as an absolute. Now, this absolute is not always applicable to the very practical problems which our agitators encounter. Marxist criticism reproached Brecht, consequently, for preaching a poor utilization of the militant element ("Never," wrote Kurella, "would the Party confide so difficult a job to so weak a person"), attributing this lack of realism to Brecht's meager revolutionary experience. They encouraged him to join the Kleinarbeit, to enroll in the school of the practical Communist. What followed showed that this advice was useless. *The Measures Taken* clearly contributed to sharpening the battle of the classes on the eve of Nazism's arrival. It caused a split in the workers' chorales whose 500,000 members were headed in the direction of reform. In the *Neue Musik* camp there was the same scandal. Their producers (with Hindemith in the lead) clearly showed that they in no way intended to go beyond their formalistic inclinations. The rupture between Brecht and Weill dates from this time. The hour of choice had struck.

After a silence of two years, Brecht and Hans Eisler (who had already composed the bare score for *The Measures Taken*) staged *The Mother*, adapted from Gorki's famous novel. Written for actors and a proletarian public, the play describes and salutes the flowering of a new human type. Lacking personal experience of revolutionary combat, Brecht takes his inspiration from that of the Russian proletariat. For the first time he tackles an epic subject, and the beauty with which he enhances the obscure exploits of the Sormowo workers equals that of "the royal plays of bygone times." The workers of Berlin, and then of the whole world, found in it a very new pleasure linked to their everyday knowledge of the battle of the classes. It is the pleasure of watching from a distance and without danger, this leisure which alone permits reflection on the representation of events as astonishing as they are familiar. This pleasure is all the more lively because Brecht gives a hint of the final victory. Humor, as he will later say, is the rising of classes. The spectator (at least the worker) can amuse himself here, and even very delicately; but while amusing himself, he is instructed, sharpening his wits and his know-how. He learns to recognize his worst enemies, those within his own ranks who are always trying to induce him to resign himself to the "lesser evil." Without pedantry, Brecht gives him a lesson in economy, implied in the action and made more explicit by the chorus.

Pelagea Wlassova, the mother of a young revolutionary worker, finds herself in unending misery. Her household crafts and her maternal concern are of no help to her. These virtues will bear fruit only after a radical conversion. She performs her first revolutionary act not through conviction, but in order to save her son. This is the beginning of a long and difficult liberation which forces her to go beyond her private universe and to see things in a larger perspective and on a grand scale. Her maternal instincts are, to a certain extent, the prime mover of her conscience. It broadens and this enlargement is perhaps Brecht's most precious contribution to socialist thought. He foresees that, in the school of daily combat, workers will be transformed into technicians of politics. All his work favors a constant control of the directional functions by the masses.

With the love of Pelagea Wlassova for her son, Brecht introduces a new theme into his work. Until that time, it had been dominated by a strange rupture with the bonds of parenthood. The Brechtian heroes had undergone so profound a mutilation that their mothers no longer recognized them. Now, in *The Mother* maternal love intervenes to resolve the antinomies of sexual love that Brecht had unceasingly proclaimed to be without issue or duration. Henceforth, it will leave its imprint upon Brechtian heroes from Mother Carrar to Grusche in *The*

Caucasian Chalk Circle. Everything happens as if the trauma, produced by Brecht's rupture with his family and his past, was beginning to clear up. The result, perhaps, is this delicacy and restraint in the expression of his sentiments.

> THE MOTHER: You are always hearing it said that
> mothers are soon done losing their sons, but I,
> I have saved mine. How did I save him?
> By the third thing.
> He and I, we were two, but the third
> thing, the common thing, communally
> pursued, that's the thing
> that united us,
> a great thing, common to many men.

Courtly love was already beginning to conflict with the third term, mystic faith. Brecht transferred this conflict from the paternal to the fraternal. Man and woman are engaged in a common action (and no longer a contemplation). Their love battles dialectically with a more universal sentiment: friendship, friendship for all the oppressed, who are their brethren. This reevaluation causes, in part, the novelty of Brecht's lyricism. The poet no longer expresses himself in terms of an image (subjective) of the loved woman, but of shared becoming and experience. In this sense, it can be said that Helene Weigel (whom he married two years before writing *The Mother*) is omnipresent in the work of Brecht. She is not eulogized, but implied in all those roles that he conceived for her, with her, and to which she gave her life.

But, at the same time, death, as well as love, takes on a new meaning. That of Pawel Wlassov is not lonely. Certainly, it is tragic, but useful and forward-looking. The executioners are no longer accursed, being of the same flesh as the victim and, like him, susceptible to the rule of the conscience. The tragedy, at a degree of extreme tension, carries with it the seed of its own dissolution. It teaches the oppressed not to be their own assassins any longer.

Brecht's conversion, however, did not proceed without interior conflict. In *Saint Joan of the Stockyards* (1930), he makes an effort to dispose of the residue of his bourgeois education. The violence which he had just stated to be the tragic condition of an effective humanity had not yet succeeded in gaining Brecht's intimate acceptance. He was not yet able to escape the nostalgia of an impossible agreement except at the price of a cruel examination of cruel reality. Written for the five-hundredth anniversary of the death of Joan of Arc, the play is an experimental work. In it, he tried to manage new material: the crisis which had just plunged two worlds into unheard-of economic upheaval. Of course, this bold attempt posed problems of form. Brecht solved them by having ironic recourse to the language of the classical tragedy. He wanted thus to fight, *from the inside*, Schillerian idealism which continued to weigh heavily upon German letters. The Joan of Schiller, like that of Brecht, finds herself in a battle against a system where the human element, far from blooming, is injured. Joan intends to restore this human element. She is inspired by feudal values like the mysticism of the blood, divine right, etc. From this position, she opposes any rational and elective conception of the State. Working with the obscure, creative forces of nature (the people), she must submit to the imperatives of the idea (God). This she prefers, and it causes failure: "God demands a blind instrument; you can only succeed in closing your eyes. The day that you saw, God abandoned you." Only sacrifice (and not reasonable will) can change the world, and it is through suffering and renunciation that divine inspiration is manifested. In order to save the kingdom, Joan must sublimate her "too human" instincts. We can see that the tragic conflict here is interiorized.

It is not at all astonishing that Brecht criticized this idealistic concept of the story. It falsifies the role that the real Joan played in the elimination of feudal vestiges and the establishment, in France, of a national monarchy. Schiller's Joan, on the other hand, could only justify the reactionary solution of the German middle class, around 1800, to the crisis caused by the French revolution. Besides, it must have encouraged tendencies toward the obscurity of German romanticism.

That is why Brecht "updates" the character of Joan of Arc.

He transfers the scene of the tragedy to Chicago's stockyards, in the throes of unemployment and financial speculation, transforming his heroine into a militant member of the Salvation Army. He burdens her character with all the illusions of the lower middle class: believing she is helping the poor, she plays into the hands of the capitalists instead. Her heroism is only a form of drunkenness from which Brecht himself was hardly free. Not having understood that the only thing, so little and yet so difficult, would be to answer disorder with calculation and violence, Joan dies alone, useless and rejected, even by those she believed she was helping. The reign of the conscience is bitter when deprived of its effects. With Joan assassinated, the people in power take over her legend. She is deprived of her death and of the sense of her life. For the system takes over our actions, assimilates them, deforms them and utilizes them as it wishes.

Mauler himself, the powerful speculator who with a wave of his hand can deprive thousands of workers of their bread, doesn't escape this alienation. He does not stop covering his deals with humanitarian pretenses. But even if he should happen to obey some sincere impulse, it always remains inextricably connected with his interests. He is condemned, in a tragicomic way, to succeed and earn money. Mauler, at the end of the play, deplores this interior divorce in the manner of Goethe, but the poet urges him to take the responsibility for it. The irony here must be taken into consideration. There is no less irony just because the proletariat could not deliver itself from this inhuman condition except by overturning the system. The paradox is that it is up to the contradictory man to suppress the contradictions. And there is no way to succeed in doing this except through sacrifice. So Brecht, at the same time he is denouncing the absurdity of sacrifice, gives it a meaning. To the useless sacrifice of Joan, he opposes the unspectacular sacrifice of an old working woman beaten up by the strikebreakers. For the good act is not the one which exalts and ameliorates its author, but the one which improves, even modestly, the world.

Life always anticipates the language involved. Brecht has

recourse to the indirect instrument of parody to underline the anachronisms of a certain morality.

MAULER: Slift, is this the way you conducted the fight I entrusted to you?

SLIFT: You may have my head for it!

MAULER: What good's your head to me? I'll take your hat! That's worth a dollar.

It is worth the trouble to see why this comeback sparks laughter. It is because in a godless society, in which the conjugal notions of sacrifice and of ritual punishment have disappeared, a man's head is worth less than his hat. The capitalistic relation between employer and employee has succeeded the feudal one between lord and vassal. We are headed toward a nonviolent objectivization of human relationships. Money plays the role of substitute or image. Consequently, the notion of personal, bloody vengeance seems very "literary" to us today. Hence our laughter is a laugh of surprise. In this instance our daily experience is judging an outmoded rhetoric which, however, we have not stopped using. Our laughter places us at a distance and that is what Brecht calls an "effect of alienation."

If Brecht has recourse to irony, it is because he is still lacking a new language. Or rather let us say that his knowledge of social mechanisms is still insufficient. The great capitalists and the lower middle class are extremely individualized here, but their proletarian adversaries remain submerged in the collective anonymity of the chorus. This lack of balance limits the universality of the tragedy. It could be called an unsuccessful attempt to found a new classicism (classic means that which is self-sufficient, the closed and perfect microcosm). But one can counter this by saying that the limitations and contradictions in *Saint Joan of the Stockyards* reflect those of a contradictory and limited age. By 1932 fascism had invaded cultural life. No German theater agreed to produce the play. Brecht's hour of exile was approaching.

Terror forces man to make extreme choices. Brecht was to demonstrate this in one of his last didactic plays, *The Exception and the Rule* (1930). It is a cold, faultless demonstration.

A merchant has to cross the desert in the company of a guide and a native porter. The police no longer protect him and he is afraid. He is afraid of the desert and of the slaves who, being poorly paid and maltreated, should logically turn on him. He is going to try to divide them. But the guide (contrary to the porter-workman) is a union member. He can "discuss," he knows the route and foresees what is going to happen. He divines the motives of his adversary and distrusts his familiarities. Consciously proletarian, he is a rough, early outline of Matti. The merchant has a presentiment of the danger and dismisses the guide. Henceforth, his terror and brutality only increase. Lost and dying of thirst, he finally kills his porter, when the latter is offering him something to drink.

The play ends with the trial of the murderer. The verdict: "The accused acted in a legitimate state of self-defense: it makes little difference whether he was *actually* threatened or only *believed* himself to be menaced. In such a situation, he *should* believe himself threatened. The accused is acquitted." The reasoning is most cynical. The victim is caught in the gears of a merciless class logic. In a murderous system, murder is the rule. Not to avenge oneself, to return good for evil, is an exception; and justice does not take exceptions into account. And besides, if the porter did not kill his master, it is not from kindness, but through fear. His ignorance of the social rules condemns him. It in no way enters Brecht's mind to discuss the verdict. All classes in power institute, according to him, rules that conform to their interests. In *The Measures Taken* it is the interest of the revolutionary proletariat; in *The Exception and the Rule* it is the interest of the landed class. Whoever excludes himself from the rule points up the exception. Any antisocial attitude is a guilty attitude in Brecht's universe. But while the rule of the merchant aims at maintaining the exploitation of some men by others, the one upon which *The Measures Taken* is based implies a transformation of the system and a suppression of violence. Brecht, in spite of his moral relativism, is not impartial. He protests (and encourages us to protest) against the established rule in the name of a future set of rules.

He proposes a transitory, provisional set of rules to denounce the rules of the past and show that they can be modified.

> May everything called habitual disturb us
> Find abuse in the rules
> And everywhere that abuse shows up
> Find the remedy for it.

Here Brecht is defining the method that he would like to see applied to social relationships. "Art," he was to say much later, "is always impotent in the face of individual or general catastrophes (desire for power, love, war, etc.). Art remains defeatist when confronted with human nature." [2] Science, on the other hand, refuses to consider as natural the cataclysms of nature like drought or epidemics. At this point, the distance Brecht has progressed can be measured. In his first plays, he was fascinated by the enigma of social acts. These acts surpass us, lead us far beyond our avowed intentions, and sometimes even destroy us. But in consequence, Brecht puts the unknown factors of human behavior in parentheses, knowing that we still lack the scientific tools which would allow the determination of its laws. Wherever the scientist is still asking questions, the writer cannot yet speak out. Human nature interests Brecht only to the extent that he can transform it.

Brecht could be reproached for enclosing his characters in a mechanical universe without liberty or escape. *The Exception and the Rule* implies, in effect, neither good nor bad men, but one who exploits and two who are exploited, trapped in a dialectic of terror.

> Two men have conquered the river:
> only one will emerge the victor.
> When I say *we*, it is something other
> than *you* and *I*.
> We conquer the river
> and you conquer me.

This dialectic will open up on liberty only much later. "We," cries out a character in *The Days of the Commune*, "is much more than you and I."

2 Interview in *Le Monde*, June 25, 1955.

6 · Practical Truth

Round Heads and Pointed Heads · *Five Difficulties in Writing the Truth* · *Fear and Misery in the Third Reich* · *Señora Carrar's Rifles* · *The Trial of Lucullus*

> We were cutting across the battle of the classes
> Changing countries more often than shoes.
>
> TO POSTERITY

AFTER 1933 Brecht was not to stop running from the armies of his own country; he was chased from Vienna to Paris, to Denmark, into Finland, and finally to the United States, where he found relative security. In the first years of his exile his production became somewhat more sparse. He was absorbed in immediate tasks like meetings, writings for certain occasions, and, above all, the problems of survival. All he carried along with him in his baggage was the theatrical technique he had just developed and which he would henceforth use as an effective weapon. The bywords of the revolutionary movement were to guide him through growing confusion and solitude. He would remain, for fifteen years, faithful to his people although everything—distance and thought—separated him from them. He unceasingly spoke of them with tenderness and anger. Their answer could come only with his return from exile when Brecht submitted his works to the test of the stage in a situation where the instruments of production were finally in the hands of the producers.

The first plays of this period were polemical. And yet in them it is evident that the rough outlines of new themes were developing. But they would come into full bloom only in the great works of his maturity. This was a period of transition and research. Hence, *Round Heads and Pointed Heads* (1932) has a fragmentary character, lacking homogeneity. This satire of

Hitlerism is little more than a labored nothing. But while Hitlerism caught most German intellectuals off guard, Brecht gave a clairvoyant analysis of it from the very beginning. Nazism could only impose itself with the complicity of industrial and financial capital, of the military aristocracy, and of the middle class, all three of which were being menaced by the revolution. This is demonstrated by Brecht with the help of an allegory which he situates in the imaginary kingdom of Jahoo. Fearing the revolt of debt-ridden peasants, the rich landowners resort to the services of Iberin, the man of the hour. The allusion is transparent. He is pointing out the material cause of the war of the classes by substituting a very vulgar myth for them. Iberin, knowing that the people are "little inclined to abstractions," gives them a palpable enemy. He divides humanity into the round heads and the pointed heads, accusing the latter of spoiling the kingdom. It is a clever method of dividing the poor and preventing them from making any claims. A street scene shows up the vanity of subterfuge. There the little people nourish the most contradictory hopes. They expect Iberin to satisfy the proprietor and the tenant at the same time, to raise and lower the price of bread, and in short, to suppress the unending conflicts of the middle classes without suppressing them.

The demonstration, as correct as it may be, suffers from a certain stylized quality. Wanting to reincarnate what is known as the great man in history, Brecht, like so many others, fails. His Iberin-Hitler lacks depth. He is a concept and not a character. This is so true that even the least important shopkeeper in this play is more alive than he. Doubtless, there is an inherent difficulty in any "epic" representation of history, whose anachronism, in any case, Brecht already senses. Trying to individualize social conflicts, he collides with unforeseen problems. If he wants to illustrate certain moral contradictions in the capitalistic system in a living manner, his character Nana fits very badly into the action of the play. She expresses, in a lyric strain, Brecht's intimate misgivings, a job he willingly entrusts to prostitutes. Hence, the structure of the play lacks equilibrium, Nana remaining its dross to some extent.

Hunger forces Nana to denounce the rich Jew Guzmann, who had previously taken advantage of her, to the Nazis. The trial, however, goes against her. The lawyer's case illustrates astonishingly well the role that a capitalistic society allocates to sex. It shows the love of Guzmann to be noble and passionate and attributes a basely interested sexuality to Nana.

> Sirs, impenetrable are human actions.
> The authors themselves don't know their causes
> and the closest scrutiny could not separate them
> from inexplicable obscurity. One finds a being
> and loves him. Another wants to love
> and looks for a being. So one loves
> the beloved and the other loves love. In one case
> it's destiny and in the other it's being in heat.

Evidently Brecht refutes this dissociation, refusing, as he was to say in his poem on Empedocles, "to obscure any further what is already obscure in itself." To his way of thinking, each human relationship is founded on an exact economy, and because of this, miracles are excluded. Nana has to be a prostitute instead of Isabelle, who flees into a convent to escape the advances of an ignoble lieutenant of Iberin. In the last analysis, Nana pays for everything; it is a forced sacrifice and the most idealized language only serves to veil the hypocrisy of a system in which the purest sentiments are deformed.

Besides, Nazism, in perfecting the technique of lying, only accelerates this degeneration of language. Brecht denounces it in a clandestine manifesto which he addressed in 1935 to German intellectuals (*Five Difficulties in Writing the Truth*). He bases it on a traditional postulate which is universally accepted: the author ought to speak the truth. The social consequences which result from it, however, are as new as they are inexorable. "Whoever wants to fight lies and ignorance today," he writes, "whoever wants to speak the truth must surmount at least five difficulties. He must have the *courage* to speak the truth when

it is everywhere stifled; the *intelligence* to recognize it when
it is everywhere hidden; the *art* to make it manageable like
a weapon; the *judgment* to choose those who will know how
to make it effective and finally enough *guile* to make them
understand it. These difficulties are great for those who write
under fascism; they are also very real for those who were exiled
or who fled and even for those who write under the regime of
bourgeois liberty." Brecht does not hide the fact that these difficulties can be surmounted only at the price of "engagement" or
renunciation of the complete and total person. Whoever refuses
to deceive the weak and flatter the strong sees himself condemned to weakness, solitude, and impotence. But while Christianity leaves a *victim* to answer "I am the truth" to the question "What is truth?" Brecht states that "the good are never
defeated because of their kindness, but because of their weakness." The nuance is important. For Brecht a conquered virtue
is a bad virtue. So virtue can conquer, at least under certain
conditions.

Brecht's truth is at the same time subjective (what I can
seize of it according to my situation and my intelligence) and
objective (what I make of it, what society makes of it). One
cannot capture it for himself alone. It is graven in the facts, and
he inscribes it there. It interprets his dialectical relationship to
the world very exactly. It is a job and not a possession. Brecht's
truth aims at only one goal: to allow man to manage, dominate,
and direct the world (*die Welt handhabbar machen*). Many
writers today are content to propound useless truths. In doing
this, they "resemble painters who brush still lifes on the sides of
a scrapped ship." Now Brecht urges them to give importance
to things that are important. For him art is on display. An
author must then 1] know how to choose his truths and 2] how
to situate them in the whole and give them sense. This science exists: it is dialectical materialism, the science of contradiction and change. It will be noted in passing that Brecht no
longer subordinated the truth to the party or even to the proletariat. The party and the proletariat, here, are only means to
an end which surpasses them. What end? It is the establishment

of a more just relationship between man and men and between men and nature.

These are its practical consequences. To write is—and is only —a social act. Careful of his interlocutor (who, in a divided society, is no more immutable than abstract), the writer will constantly let his vocabulary be subjected to criticism. The lie always affects a noble, evasive, general language. The language of truth, on the other hand, is dry, precise, and statistical. From all this "complex" which obscures it, he disengages the little naked fact which fights, all by itself, all the lies in the world: "In our time, whoever, instead of *people* says *population*, instead of *land* says *basic property* is already avoiding the perpetuation of many lies. He removes the adulterated magic from words. Whoever brings out the odor and color of the earth favors the lies of its owners. For the question is not one of the productivity of the land nor of the love that men have for it, nor even of their efforts, but essentially of the market for grains and the cost of labor."

Thus, at a time when political language was tending to become exalted, Brecht indicated the concrete means of combating a crisis whose causes are essentially economic. Fascism appears each time that a democratic bourgeoisie resorts, despairing of the cause, to illegality. Fascism, then, is a product of capitalism, and people cannot combat one without combating the other. The phenomenon is "at once old and new," and it is only the "most naked, cynical, oppressive, and lying form of capitalism." Whoever accuses a mythical Germany instead of the system only prepares the way for war.

So, unlike so many of his exiled compatriots, Brecht does not renounce his origins at all. "Must one make up his mind," he wrote, "to be German no longer? Will hell disappear if I'm good?" The beginnings of the ethics of *Galileo* are evident here. All men are responsible for the inhumane. There is no salvation for them as long as evil exists.

Brecht applies this practical truth in *Fear and Misery in the Third Reich*, which he composed between 1935 and 1938 from clandestine stories and reports. In it, he studies the decomposition of German society through its common symptoms. At this convulsive stage, he finds, the monstrosity of the capitalistic system bursts into broad daylight. It is the age, announced in *The Exception and the Rule*, "when the arbitrary has the force of law, when humanity dehumanizes itself." It is true that the Brechtian characters, who are prisoners in this hell, are no longer in a position to grasp the absurdity of it. The bourgeois values which had been their frame of reference until that time have become useless. Paternal authority, the family, law, professional honesty, the teaching of the church, in short this whole network of habits and securities was breaking up. Distrust was universal; henceforth, indirect discourse would be the rule. Every human relationship was being poisoned by the invisible presence of a third person: the *Führer*, the symbol of permanent menace and accusation. Then each person had to play a sinister comedy with himself and his neighbors, keeping his distance and cutting himself in two—a symptom of organized schizophrenia. And yet everyone continued to cling to outmoded words. Notwithstanding, there was no longer in this disjointed, pathological universe either common measure or common language.

THE WIFE: I don't understand you. You're not going to speak to me like that, are you? You would think that I am the police in person.

THE HUSBAND: Everyone is suspect. It's enough for there to be a suspicion for everyone to be suspect.

Incapable of grasping the real causes of their misery, the Brechtian lower middle classes accuse the rain, politics, the Jews, and the people who are poorer than they. But the higher one climbs in the social hierarchy, the more complicated and refined the hypocrisy becomes. Alibis multiply; the lie grows in proportion to the culture. A Jewish woman, the wife of an eminent professor, breaks down in the midst of her packing:

THE WIFE: During this last hour that we have, I don't want us not to have the courage to look each other in the eye. Don't tell me not to leave. I am hurrying for I don't want you to have the time to say to me: Go! It's a question of days, weeks. Character is like a glove that lasts a certain length of time. There are good ones which last a long time. But none lasts forever.

Nothing can any longer veil this couple's divisions, fear, and absence of love and solidarity. The only solution, cleverly suggested by Brecht, would be to renounce honors and comfort and flee together to combat this inhuman system. But in fact, our professor could not even discuss such a thing. Too many interests hold him there and make him an accomplice to it all. From then on what good would the best "character" (in the bourgeois sense) be to him? He lavishes many timid assurances on his wife and on himself, and betrayal has already cast its dice.

If the working class itself does not escape this generalized demoralization, certainly some workers fight it with a sure instinct for the truth. An old worker before a microphone is being exploited for the propaganda of the regime. Carefully observing the popular idiom (of which he grasps the logic and not, like so many others, the picturesque element), Brecht reproduces this uneven battle. The reporter completes, deforms, and drowns the timid assertions of his interlocutor who, nevertheless, makes an effort to slip a few rudiments of truth under the noses of the manager and the SA henchman.

THE REPORTER: You mean, my friend, that under the old system the workers hardly had the desire to laugh. People used to say "Why work?", isn't that right?
THE WORKER: There are some people who say that.

Here we find the application of the ruse that Brecht was preaching in his *Five Difficulties*. Can ruse conquer ruse? The lie in the last scene seems destined to triumph forever. A few hunted militants are listening to the radio. Hitler has just entered Vienna and he is jubilant.

THE OLD WORKER: Each time you hear them yowling that way, you must admit that they give the impression of becoming stronger all the time. Wouldn't you say that it's really *one* people?
THE WOMAN: You'd say they were twenty thousand drunkards who had just been given money for beer.

THE YOUNG WORKER: Perhaps we're the only ones to say that.
THE WOMAN: Yes, us and people like us.

This dry, firm language is more than ruse; it's the language
of faith.

Yet, Brecht had never been more alone than in these years,
1936–1938. Already his people could no longer hear his voice.
The torturers had made them into a unanimous puppet. Germany was ripe for war. From this time on, Brecht addressed
other countries, trying to ward off the inevitable.

But first, here are a few words about *Señora Carrar's Rifles*.
In it, Brecht transplants the theme of *The Mother* into civil
war Spain. A play by Synge (*Riders to the Sea*) gave him his
inspiration, and for Brecht it was a chance to criticize, through
the inner conflicts of a mother who has just lost her son, a certain mystique of death, which was held to be fatal. The problem
posed by Synge is taken up in a concrete context; his "poetic"
theater is corrected. From this brief outline, one will remember
the dialogue in which a revolutionary worker and a miserable
priest confront each other. In it Christian nonviolence is sternly
taken to task.

The Trial of Lucullus, written on the eve of the war, seems
to me, despite its brevity, a decisive work. Brecht renounces the
schematic setup of the didactic plays. When the catastrophe is
imminent, Brecht's lyricism, by a curious paradox, bursts suddenly into bloom. Never had the world of the living appeared
more desirable than in those hours before the war. One would
say that Brecht, having reached forty, relaxes. This finally acquired ease is expressed, not without humor, in "A Little Organum for the Theater" (1948), in which Brecht sums up his
theories. "Our job," he writes, "is to divert the children of the
scientific age, to speak to their senses and to amuse them. We
can't insist strongly enough upon this point, for we Germans
are only too tempted by abstraction. With us, sexual pleasure
becomes a conjugal duty and we don't expect art to please but
to instruct. We justify our acts not by the pleasure they bring
us, but by the sweat they cost us." He reminds us that the theater
is a luxury, and that man, in the last analysis lives only for the

superfluous. He concludes that art is the lightest and the most delicate form of existence.

Lucullus is an elegiac play, perhaps the only one that Brecht ever wrote. All nostalgia is elegiac. That includes the longing for what was, what will be, or what might be. Actually, the elegy is a form of escape or evasion. It is accompanied by a melancholy that Brecht, however, is prepared to dominate. Even though the harmony with the world (this harmony that all poets pursue) is inaccessible to him, Brecht takes up the burden of the world with all its conflicts. His technique of alienation no longer serves him even in criticizing the untruthful forms of human relationships. It brings to light the unique, irreplaceable character of existence. In the ordinary and the regular, there is so constant a miracle that you could almost speak of a *holy* meaning in life. Because war attacks this holiness, Brecht condemns his Lucullus. Being founded on a profound respect for life, this verdict is just. This respect and love inspired a eulogy of the cherry tree that Lucullus brought back from Asia.

THE PEASANT: It husbands the land.
LUCULLUS: But it has difficulty standing up to the wind.
THE PEASANT: The red cherries have more meat.
LUCULLUS: But the black ones are sweeter.

THE PEASANT: Friends, of all that the bloody war,
Abominable to our memory, has conquered,
That is the best! For this little tree lives.
Something new and friendly
is mixed into the growing, active grapes and the raspberry bushes
with growing generations to offer them its fruits. I salute you, you
to whom we owe it all. When all the booties
of both Asias will have returned to dust,
each year, the living will see once again
the most beautiful of your trophies floating
in the springtime breeze, covering the hills
with its white flowering.

This dialogue is like a happy pause in the inexorable unwinding of the trial. Even from the bosom of human divisions, a clear, delicate note rises with a gesture of confidence and the fragile seeds of the harmony to come. Certainly, anguish still exists, but it is under control. Individual death seems to be absorbed by the life force of generations, which are linked to one another in a mysterious solidarity. But the value of our individual existence is not denied. If Lucullus is condemned, it is precisely for having "sent so many beings to the kingdom of shadows before their allotted time was up." The tribunal which judges him is perhaps only the nocturnal voice of our consciences. These dead "who don't have hands for taking, nor mouths for eating" become the advocates of all the living who have mouths and nothing to eat and of all the mutilated existences, stems without flowers, to whom we are indebted for a more humane world. They judge us, but the criteria of their judgment are not those of History. Their beyond is that of an unwritten history, "a history of the beaten," that Brecht substitutes for the one which consecrates warrior heroes and inscribes their names on the tablet of the immortals. In this official historiography the defeated are made to say what people want them to say. Lucullus invokes it in his defense. But it is very much in vain, for the defeated are invited to express themselves. Those who, in their all too short existence, have learned patience, those who see themselves constrained, not to choose but to submit to their destiny, all the unheroic whose humble work was yet so useful, all the slaves, the soldiers, and the mothers who saw their sons taken from them come to denounce the vanity of military conquest. Their questions are anything but lyric. They are as dry as a household budget. Who took from whom? Who gave what? The scale of values is reversed. Only his weaknesses could reprieve a Lucullus, these weaknesses which appear "like empty spaces in the chain of his violence." Then the gluttony of Lucullus is called to account, the gluttony which made it possible for a cook to perfect his art and which was worth the cherry tree to Italy. But the tribunal judges consider that progress is too costly. For it is not true that culture suffices to justify the misery of the greatest number. The selective, aristocratic conception of culture is here rejected, and with it, war.

THE JUDGE OF THE DEAD: May he disappear into nothingness;
so much violence and conquering ambition
never amassed but one single empire,
the empire of shadows.

The play was not produced until 1950 in East Berlin. Brecht
and Dessau converted it into an opera with the clearer title:
The Condemnation of Lucullus. Following a controversy with
the Minister of Popular Culture, Brecht made a few changes
which set tongues wagging in the West German press. He
corrected the unconditional pacifism of the original version,
being extremely careful to point out, and a bit laboriously at
that, that there are only bad kings and that defensive wars are
not unjust.

> Like the wolf
> who throws himself on a herd
> we have been beaten down
> in the service of an assassin.
> Why haven't we betrayed the aggressor?
> Why haven't we rejoined the defender?

This is an allusion to a burning past and a critical present. Is
it possible to discover in it resignation and perhaps even opportunism? All virtue is limited. Let us be Brechtian for Brecht too.

7 · The Actor in the Scientific Age
A Little Organum for the Theater · Theater-arbeit · The Dialectic in the Theater

> Let's take an example. A sister cries because
> her brother must go off to war. It's the war
> of the peasants and he joins the peasants.
> Should we partake completely of the sister's
> sorrow? or not at all? We ought to know
> how to share and how not to share her
> sorrow.
>
> THE DIALECTIC IN THE THEATER

BRECHT'S THEORIES are the subject of Byzantine controversies. They are set up as dogma while it is really a question of a method for action. People are astonished by their novelty, forgetting that Brecht systematized and modernized the rules that Lessing, Goethe, Schiller and, naturally, Diderot had already tried out. In order to surpass them, he took his inspiration from the research of Piscator, who aimed at setting up a "political theater"; and the "Neue Sachlichkeit" movement, which enjoyed a brief spurt during the twenties, was not without influence on him. Brecht, to say the most, takes what he needs where he finds it. Certainly, by dint of posing as a champion of "non-Aristotelian" theater, he encouraged certain misunderstandings himself. Thus it is that he came to neglect, through his interest in demonstration, the didactic aspects of ancient Greek tragedy, which is not founded solely on *catharsis* (or purification of the passions by identification with the hero) but on an *anagnorisis* (the act of becoming conscious of something) as well. One mustn't forget that the technique of the "epic theater" did not spring full-blown from the brain of Brecht. Its outlines had been forming since *The Threepenny Opera*, but it underwent successive amendments. Brecht experimented with it and perfected it on various stages in Europe and America. He defined it in his theoretical essays and in the notes which accompany most of his plays. Finally, after the war he made an effort, with his wife Helene Weigel, to build up a generation of "scientific" actors at the Berliner Ensemble.

What exactly do we mean by that? In the space of a hundred years, the machine has upset our manners of living and thinking. Perfecting and multiplying its means of production, humanity has taken over and transformed nature and pried from it long-unsuspected resources. The masses, passive and silent for centuries, are beginning to take their destinies into their own hands. Human relationships are also tending to become organized in a more rational way. Now, in the general commotion, while all man's actions are being reexamined, Brecht is the first to dream of radically correcting the *social function* of the theater. The bourgeois spectator expects the theater to furnish him with something like opium, a cheap means of exchanging his daily, unbearable, broken world for a harmonious, but illusory world. Instead of bringing a faithful and shaded representation of the real, the actor is expected to reincarnate the heroic or erotic reveries of an assemblage of sleepwalkers. In the space of an evening, the butcher wishfully dreams of becoming a king; the housewife, a whore; the accountant, an assassin. And to accomplish this magic the actor must himself enter into a trance. The actor must identify with his character (king, whore, or assassin), and the spectator with the actor. Then we say—in tones of admiration—that he "is giving it everything he's got."

Such a sacrifice, Brecht remarks, is unworthy of the scientific age. Each day science teaches us to be astounded by what exists, to criticize the world, not in a purely negative spirit, but with the end in view of changing it. To criticize an evil is to cure it; to criticize nature is to make it productive and livable. So Brecht invites theater people—authors and producers—to participate joyously and effectively, "recognizing the cause," in this effort at rational transformation, following the example given them by doctors, engineers, and manufacturers. And what must be questioned here if not the relationships between men? But to criticize something, one must be aware of it. The theater then has no other goal for Brecht than to present us with the objective image of a given society.

However, societies are not immutable. When the actor approaches the image that Shakespeare, for example, has left us of his times, he ought to do it as a historian. He is to keep his distance from the past and oppose it to the present in such a way that this present (to which we are so accustomed that it seems to "go by itself") will appear suddenly relative, strange and different from the past. The Brechtian actor is a man who astounds himself and us. He considers his role to be a stranger (in Latin: *alienus*). He becomes a contradictory personage, at once Hamlet and a critical witness of Hamlet, the present quoting and the past quoted, simultaneously expressing the sentiments of his role and his own; he is not the "sacred monster," but a man among others, suggesting to his fellow men a judgment, inviting them into a discussion and then encouraging their retorts.

According to Brecht, he resembles the witness at an accident explaining what he has seen to curious passers-by. He does not cast a spell: he demonstrates. He will know how to represent even the most violent emotions of his character without the spectator losing his faculties of observation and control. Continually alternating imitation and commentary, he will make an effort to explain to the audience how and why, according to him, such a thing has happened. He will in no way hide the fact that he has studied the event and formed an opinion about it. He will make very sure not to consider the behavior of the personage he is imitating as natural, inevitable, or in character. On the contrary, he will make the unique, surprising, exceptional quality of each of his acts stand out for the audience. For each one depends on a choice. It is only one possibility among many, an "alternative," and the actor ought to suggest this idea of alternatives. In this way, he brings the spectator around to the *facts* which are related in the drama; and, in subtly indicating the extent to which they are relative and consequently capable of modification, he subjects them to a "productive" criticism. And it is productive since it ought to move us to transform and humanize our fate.

In short, the Brechtian actor *alienates* the real (in German:

verfremden). Brecht develops a new technique for him even though it is inspired by a very ancient foreign tradition. "The Chinese actor," he writes, "watches himself act. Mimicking the unexpected appearance of a cloud, his soft and powerful unfolding, his metamorphosis, rapid though imperceptible, he turns now and again to his audience as if to say: 'It's like that, isn't it?' And throughout his performance, he observes his arms and legs, sizing up the feat they have just accomplished. Around him, the decorations are being set up and furniture is being moved around: it does not bother him in the least. Visibly, he considers himself and his role as if they were foreign to him. It is quite the contrary with someone having hallucinations!"

The Brechtian method could not be better defined although, of course, it is applied not to clouds but to social phenomena. By way of example, here is the method by which Brecht will alienate one such famous scene from Schiller. Mary Stuart, for years the prisoner of her rival, Elizabeth of England, makes a final attempt at reconciliation. She submits to the arrogance of her adversary with a humility at once sincere and forced (it is only too evident). Every word she utters vibrates with wounded pride and pent-up hatred until the moment when the storm, which has been contained too long, bursts, bringing the sinister game to a brutal end.

In order to make it possible for the actor to alienate this scene, Brecht transfers it to a prosaic setting. The queens become fishmongers, and the magic of stately verse is changed to the idiom of daily speech with this result: instead of becoming sympathetic to the plight of Mary Stuart, our attention is drawn to the mechanisms underlying her battle. Beneath the nobility of the language we discover a "disloyal competition." Mary and Elizabeth are equally bad; during years of reciprocal hatred, both have alternately resorted to violence and ruse. Here, only the situations differ. One has the other at her mercy. Now, the actor ought to bring to light the precise real facts of this *conflict of interest* (love and politics). This exercise helps him do this and, at the same time, permits him to disentangle the comic aspects from the tragic exaltation. It gives him the means to satirize his character and therein discover its contradictions.

It is unnecessary to add that the actor, if he wants to criticize the social behavior of his characters in a beautiful and intelligent manner, ought to sharpen his gifts of observation and reflection. "Putting one's heart into it" is no longer enough. "It is not possible," says Brecht, "to demonstrate something without knowing it. The actor must adapt himself to the science of human relationships, practically and experimentally by taking part in the great battle of the classes."

8 · The Temptation of Kindness

Mother Courage and Her Children · Herr Puntila and His Man Matti · The Visions of Simone Machard · The Days of the Commune · The Good Woman of Setzuan · The Caucasian Chalk Circle

BRECHT FINISHED his *Mother Courage* in 1939. War had just broken out. For six years it was going to be engulfing millions of little people. Many of them were to submit to it as if it were an inexplicable, inevitable, natural catastrophe. Brecht wanted to show them that they were really accomplices in perpetrating their own misfortunes. In this way, he allies himself to the only writer who had even an inkling of the cause of misery in seventeenth-century Germany. In fact, he even took his inspiration from two plays by Grimmelhausen: *The Adventures of Simplex Simplicissimus* (1669) and *Vagabond Courage* (1670). The two main characters survive through the Thirty Years' War, but only at the price of trickery and unheard-of suffering. But while Simplex, fired by a powerful desire and purified in flames, ends in a mystical communion, Courage, a victim of her own duplicity, ends her career degraded and accursed. But in the margin of this pietist antithesis, Grimmelhausen states some less comforting truths. For example, he writes, "Many want the war to last because war fits in with their selfish interests. Now those who are hanged are always the poor or the petty thieves. This is just, for they have arrogated to themselves the right of exercising a sublime art which is reserved for the more powerful."

It is not just by chance that German society was becoming conscious of its own divisions at this time. It had just undergone a decisive crisis after the Peasants' War. The feudal values had broken down, and no one was any longer fooled by the "holy" nature of war. The reform had borne fruit: "There remained only," writes Brecht, "cynicism and business." If Mother Courage followed first the Imperial and then the Swedish armies, it was certainly not because she had changed her convictions. Very simply, she was hoping to get her slice of the cake. This hope was shared by all the little people that Brecht re-creates. "War is order," says one of Brecht's sergeants. "In wartime only men and cattle are counted."

In the last analysis, unfortunately, this order is really only organized disorder. Mother Courage's plan is illusory. She would like to live from the war, but is not willing to give anything to it. The game will ruin her. In it she is going to lose her three children. In business (and war is only business on a grand scale) whoever wants to get out goes bankrupt. If Mother Courage hangs on, it is only from the instinct of self-preservation. Such is the tragic situation, the contradiction in the play. Brecht says of this contradiction that it "can only be surmounted by the whole society after a long and terrifying battle." [1] Evidently then, Brechtian tragedy does not exclude a certain optimism. There comes a time when Mother Courage, crushed by her misfortune, begins to have an inkling of its causes: "May war be accursed!" True, it is only a flicker, but neither grief nor experience could transform a human being if reason did not intervene to give them a meaning. "The bystanders at a catastrophe," writes Brecht, "wait in vain for the victims to discover a lesson from it. As long as the masses are only the object of politics, they will not be able to consider the events that they experience as experience, but only as destiny. Catastrophes could not instruct them any more than biology instructs the guinea pig. The playwright has to open not only the eyes of Mother Courage, but also those of the spectator."

Here Brecht puts us on guard. If Mother Courage is blind, it is not because of an excess of maternal love. From its first presentation (Zurich, 1944), bourgeois criticism missed the point. Immediately, Brecht reworked his play to modify the

[1] *The Dialectic in the Theater.*

development of his point of view. For example, Eilif takes advantage of a moment of inadvertence on his mother's part to turn himself over to the recruiting sergeant. In the first version, Mother Courage is distracted while she is offering a drink to the sergeant's companion in order to dissuade him of his project. So she surrenders her son to the war at the exact moment that she believed that, at the price of some shoddy maternal trickery, she would be able to keep him out of it. Now, in the corrected version, Mother Courage loses her son because she was selling by shrewd bargaining or because of the attraction of profit. In this way, she becomes an accomplice to the murder of her own son. In this conflict between love and interest, interest has the last word. Is Mother Courage guilty? No, she is rather vanquished by "the force of things." Whoever has no choice is not guilty. But when Mother Courage preaches resignation or when she tries to justify a bad world, then she is really guilty. And this is because the good, for Brecht, is what ameliorates. This is not the heroism which destroys heroes, but which destroys evil.

Brecht adroitly compares this morality taken from Marx [2] to that of Christianity. One of the sons of Mother Courage is shot for having refused to surrender the regiment's money box to the enemy. A complaint compares this useless sacrifice to the passion of Christ. Brecht refuses to comment on this crucifixion of the just and the innocent for the sake of the millennium. But eight scenes later he contrasts it with the death of Catherine, the deaf, simple daughter of Mother Courage. Her death is useful since Catherine, by beating a drum, saves the children of a city that the enemy is about to surprise. Catherine evidently knows that her mother is to be found in the city, but her act of love takes its place in a larger perspective than that of the bonds of blood. She goes beyond the "natural" virtues which imprison a Mother Courage. Thus "the stones themselves begin to speak" and she who possesses nothing can give everything. Brecht is only too well aware of the weakness

2 See the pages of *The Holy Family* which are devoted to Flower-of-Mary, Eugène Sue's heroine.

and duplicity of the poor, but he also knows that they alone will be able, in the final analysis, to outsmart, upset, and master the inhuman. Kindness is their only chance for liberty. And this kindness must be practical, useful, and devoted to the destruction of a world "where kindness is impossible," but which will end by transforming this world. And so the idea of sacrifice emerges intact from the criticism to which Brecht subjects all moral values. It has the force of an instinct, and its infectious power is incommensurable. It awakens in the dullards and the peasants who sacrifice Catherine the vague memory of that which is the most precious in man. They are resigned to killing her only because they themselves are afraid of dying. Already, in his turn, a young peasant raises the voice of revolt. What had appeared absurd now clears up with a new meaning, and if the dying Catherine laments, it is not for herself, but for the world and the failure of her sacrifice. The bells of the city will ring out only after her death, but the message is transmitted and that's what is important.

> People's strength was lacking and the goal
> lay very far in the distance.
> It was clearly visible, but as for me,
> I scarcely believed that I could attain it.
> That's how time has passed,
> The time that was given to me on earth.[3]
>
> *Die Kräfte waren gering. Das Ziel*
> *Lag in grosser Ferne,*
> *Es war deutlich sichtbar, wenn auch für mich*
> *Kaum zu erreichen.*
> *So verging meine Zeit*
> *Die auf Erden mir gegeben war.*

The rule says that man is a wolf toward men. In that case, he will not really be a man except in exceptional instances. So we have the case of Mother Courage whose calculations are false. That is why she becomes human only on rare occasions when, having renounced her logic (insufficient), she thinks she is wrong. Lacking knowledge, her instincts take the

3 From the poem "To Posterity."

place of reason. Her pitiful love for the parasitic chaplain is without illusions. It is based upon common interests, and yet has a little something more. Only this "something," that Brecht had until then denied, permits us to surpass necessities. He was to write one day, with his customary discretion, these surprising words:

> The moon shone throughout the night
> And the boat glided noiselessly across the water.
> We came back from afar.
> From time to time you have to abandon yourself,
> Lose your head and lose your mind . . .

We are well aware that friendship ruins us, and yet we cannot resist liking people. It is a necessity within us which nothing, neither reason nor experience, can stifle. It is something very timid and obstinate, a shoddy hope amid the misery of the world, for man needs man. But at the precise moment when we are becoming moved, Brecht calls us back to order. *Herr Puntila and His Man Matti* (1941), the only comedy that Brecht ever published, corrects the errors of *Mother Courage* but without bitterness. Taking his inspiration from a Finnish tale, Brecht, in this play, puts his muse at the disposal of robust popular humor. He invites us to laugh at social contradictions, and we laugh, knowing full well that they will not last forever.

These contradictions are personified by Puntila, the fat landowner who is human only when he is drinking. Nursing a hangover, he crushes and scoffs at those that, the evening before, he had showered with his liberalities. Puntila can only be himself while fleeing himself. His conscience is unbearable to him: it locks him up in an animal solitude when it should, on the contrary, deliver him from it. This causes him to seek out the friendship of his chauffeur Matti, a friendship which should break through the barrier between classes with no difficulty. But drunkenness is isolating. It exalts the subjectivity of the master which throws itself against the terrible objectivity of this world that he himself has created. He does not know how to make a slave not a slave. There is no love without liberty, and the kindness of Puntila remains, in the last analysis, without an object.

> PUNTILA: I would like to be sure that there is no longer a barrier between us. Tell me that there is no longer a barrier!
> MATTI: Your wish is my command.

The theme of Puntila could be compared to that, a few years earlier, of *City Lights*. But while the vagabond that Chaplin played submits to the caprices of his wealthy companion in a bewildered, passive, disarmed way, Brecht's Matti is already a critical and conscious proletarian. "Am I doing the right thing to drink with him?"; "Must I sleep with his daughter?": He puts all sorts of questions to himself and resolves them with common sense that is being unceasingly sharpened by experience. Distrust is not natural; it is learned, and Matti gives his workman public a lesson in distrust. Puntila willingly displays idealism. To speak of money seems vulgar to him. For him, his flights of lyricism are a means of hiding—and of hiding from himself—his real situation. He is noble in his words, but ignoble in his actions. But in his insolent answers, Matti does more than express the thoughts of his class. He is even the voice of reality, of this sober, objective, and unacceptable reality that Puntila would prefer to ignore. From this point forward, their dialogue is like one between two deaf persons:

> PUNTILA: Matti, are you my friend?
> MATTI: No.
> PUNTILA: Good, I thought so.

They can not even get together on the meaning of words. The drunken Puntila wants, for example, to hire some workers. He proposes "bonds of friendship" to them, but they prefer a "contract." He offers them a "home"; they want a "house." And when Puntila, at the height of drunkenness, decides to distribute his wealth, Matti realistically denounces utopia: "I am not going to advise you. But you would be quickly ruined, and you would soon have to close up shop."

In fact though, Puntila is more nearly free to be kind than Matti is to profit from his kindness. Worlds separate them, and this division comes abruptly to the surface on the level of love. Puntila is a son of Baal. His vitality can be attractive, but according to Brecht, it is the attraction of a crocodile. His fortune takes the place of charm for him, and if he pretends to take an interest in the troubles of a girl working in a drugstore or of a milk maid, it is only to do a better job seducing them; the moment our Don Juan sobers up he quickly betrays his real motives: "I forbid you to use the word love. It is the synonym for beastliness and nothing more. I want none of that on my farm. You can't love tomatoes and the herdsman at the same time. . . ."

Eva, his daughter, and Matti are, to a certain extent, attracted to each other. Eva, a little egotistic beast, full of false ideas, feminine but in an authoritarian way, is really quite agreeable. But since she is sensual by nature, her education is nothing more than a veneer. She retains only what can be useful to her, preparing to commit still worse blunders. The birth of this love is delicately suggested by Brecht, but it is only done to show that love is more than a blossoming. It is cultivated; it is a daily economic battle with two beings in conflict with a world hostile to love.

PUNTILA: Eva's got her faults; she's going to get fat; Okay, but not before thirty.

MATTI: Who's talking about getting fat? I say that she is not practical and would not make the right kind of wife for a chauffeur.

Yet, Eva is good-natured. Free from the imbecile attaché that she in no way wanted to marry and slightly high from a few glasses of wine, she bursts out with a heartfelt plea: "My good Matti, take me for your wife, I beg you, so that I shall have a man like the others. I don't think myself in any way superior to the others, as you may think perhaps, and I shall remain with you even through hard times." The desire for reconciliation, which motivates all the characters of the play from time to time, here attains an almost heartrending acuteness. And yet neither Eva's good will nor her love is enough. Matti makes her take a test: will she be capable of being his wife? This examination is negative. It denounces the bankruptcy of the bourgeois educational system. But, with the same blow, he condemns the conditions causing the hard lives of the working women, these "proletarians of the proletarians."

This scene should be compared to the beautiful poem which Brecht dedicated to his wife and her career as an actress. It will then be evident that he in no way rejects love, but only amorous drunkenness. The aesthetics of passion are rejected; the person loved is "tested" (erprobt), and then only is he eulogized. Thus Brecht's lyricism, far from excluding beauty, includes a critique of beauty. An example of this is the scene in which Puntila and Matti scale an imaginary mountain erected amid the alcohol fumes. It is lifted from *Mahagonny* in such a way that the distance Brecht has progressed becomes evident. Puntila exalts, but it is Matti who produces the mountain. Puntila enjoys things because they belong to him, but Matti who possesses nothing, could not share his emotion. Here, poetry appears to be an addition to possession. And it is a lie to the extent that this possession is illegitimate. Puntila's emotion is beautiful, but the moral criticism of this emotion, suggested by a few ironic words, is still more beautiful.

Abandoning chronological order we shall now proceed to *The Visions of Simone Machard* (1941–1944) and *The Days of the Commune* (1948–1949), two plays which Brecht situates in France. This country, which welcomed him at the beginning of his exile and which he was to see again just before his death, awakens in him a strange nostalgia. There he found an intangible abandon or sweetness of life. Yet his friendship is clairvoyant. He loves a certain France, but which one? Actually, *Simone Machard* only poses the question. And it is certainly not by chance that Brecht interrogates France in its darkest hour while it is in the throes of an exodus and a debacle, seeing its old dream of glory crumble.

> SIMONE: Must we still fight when the enemy has already won?
> THE ANGEL: Isn't there any wind tonight?
> SIMONE: Yes.
> THE ANGEL: Isn't there a tree in the courtyard?
> SIMONE: Yes, the poplar.

THE ANGEL: Doesn't the wind move the leaves?
SIMONE: Yes, you can hear it.
THE ANGEL: Then you must continue to fight after the enemy
has won.

This apparition of an angel in Brecht's work is likely to be
found surprising. The reason for it is that the little servant girl
has read the story of Joan of Arc. And so we see her dreaming
in her unreasonable and childish way of reenacting the exploits
of her spiritual sister who lived five centuries ago. Her dreams
cause an eruption in the real pattern of events, hiding the trail
so to speak, and metamorphosing her daily surroundings into a
grimacing, golden legend. Why does Brecht have recourse to
this dreamlike hallucination? Possibly Brecht, for critical reasons, wanted to adopt the techniques of a certain "poetic
theater," an offshoot of expressionism. Zuckmayer, with whom
he is often contrasted, was making an effort at the same time to
ennoble episodes of the resistance by giving them a metaphysical bearing.[4] Such could evidently not be what Brecht proposed
to do. He borrows from Christian imagery in order to show
that it is anachronistic. When Simone Machard distributes her
superiors' merchandise to the refugees or sets fire to a gasoline
dump that they were getting ready to turn over to the Germans,
she is being inspired by the exterior manifestations of Joan's
heroism. But this heroism collides with the conspiracy of the
very same people who taught it to her. Her martyrdom is even
ridiculous. Simone does not end up at the stake but in a lunatic
asylum. In the eyes of her masters, who soon discovered in the
former enemy an ally of their class, her case has pathological
causes. But Brecht shows us that in a sick society, the sickness
of a Simone Machard is the seed of health and reason. For,
through her delirium, Simone discovers that this France that
she had been told was a unity is, on the contrary, very badly
divided. There is one false France of the masters and another
for which she is responsible, that of the poor, the oppressed, who
are her brethren. Then it is really this delirium which dictates

4 Above all, *The Song in the Furnace*.

Simone's decisions, leading her along the path to a constantly more reasonable behavior which, in a sense, is more "adult."

What is strange is that these immersions in the subconscious are accompanied by a veritable decomposition of language. Simone's guardian angel holds forth in a curious language in which we can discover snatches of political jargon or burlesque vestiges of diurnal conversations. These deformities in Brecht's work provide the wherewithal for reflection. In a disjointed society which is deprived of a common language, Simone Machard painfully discovers new words which might be able to orient her. They are fragile and incomplete in proportion to the childishness of her conscience. But they are strong enough to brave the lies of an official terminology which speaks of honor in a time of dishonor, of reconciliation in a society irreconcilably divided. So without a doubt, Brecht intentionally situates this unveiling, unique among all his works, in a country where the language has attained, over the course of centuries, a degree of incomparable subtlety, but also of extreme vulnerability. The crafty question that Mme. Soupeau, the boss, puts to Simone Machard, "Do you at least know what France is?" initiates a total revision of political vocabulary. Brecht pursues it with still more clarity and force in *The Days of the Commune*, perhaps the most impersonal of all his plays.

As an heir of Büchner, who wrote *The Death of Danton*, Brecht makes an effort with this play to clarify the dialectic of an event whose lesson the German Marxists had ferreted out a long time before Brecht did. The novelty is that this dialectic succeeds in *reincarnating* the lesson with sure-handed art. Here, the common people are no longer content to submit passively to history; instead, they make it, becoming conscious of their historical role; and their actions, and even their errors, are still relevant today. The Commune, although abortive, appears to us today as the laboratory in which the weapons of world revolution were forged. It announces the setting sun of heroes and heroic history. The great men, the officials like Bismarck or Thiers, were reduced to ridiculous matchstick figures—perhaps too ridiculous—marionettes. They gesticulate in their slippers, these sanguinary defenders of a class that was dying. For the defeat makes the divisions burst into full view in France. For the middle class the war had "exhausted all the possibilities for business," but to the proletariat it brought a class conscience. Misery divides the poor, but when extreme enough it unites them. Not being able to obtain from her tenant the rent that she owes to her masters, the superintendent Cabet has no other choice but to join the political demonstrators who are denouncing the abettors of their common misery.

> As long as we were weak, you
> made laws to control us.
> Henceforth, these laws will be no longer observed
> as long as we no longer wish to be controlled.

The infidelity to the old laws, founded on violence, is manifested in the members of the Commune by a fidelity to coming laws and to human becoming. The popular instinct joins the instinct of Antigone. Yet this instinct does not succeed in modifying the order of events. It remained a utopia and events were not long in violently disillusioning it.

Why this failure? Brecht shows us that its causes were first of all objective. The Commune was isolated and cut off from the provinces. And this is the reason for its insoluble contradictions, from which not even the most clever intellect could find an escape. How could nighttime work be curtailed when all day long the apprenticed bakers were on guard duty? How could salaries be raised when the national guard had to be equipped? Suddenly the revolution seemed to involve great patience. But the masses were properly impatient. They were interested only in being intoxicated by a liberty which was menaced as soon as it had been acquired. Their exaltation was deadly. It fell apart when confronted with the craftiness of a middle class which possessed the experience of power and which knew how to bide its time. "The dissolute mob," said Thiers, "doesn't hesitate at blowing everything up. But the reason is plain: it possesses nothing. For the government, for us, Paris is not a symbol, but a property. Setting fire to the city does not mean defending it."

And yet it is in the furnace of its own contradictions that the revolution forged its method of combat. On the one hand, the idealists, prisoners of bourgeois legality, were repugnant to violence (this violence that the enemy imposes on them); on the the other hand, there were the partisans of an armed revolution who preached the march on Versailles, the expropriation of banks and, in short, the complete overthrowal of the system. These contradictions could be fruitful:

GENEVIEVE: We are not united. That is a bad sign.

LANGEVIN: No, it's a good sign: there is movement; but the movement must be headed in the right direction.

What followed was to show that this movement, for the time being, was erroneous. The victory of the idealists plunged the Commune into disaster. Just the same, Brecht gives this disaster a sense which is anything but tragic. A strange happiness is mixed with the sadness of the spectators and the characters alike. It is the happiness that comes from recognizing an error which means that the error can be avoided.

GENEVIEVE: Why did we fool ourselves?

LANGEVIN: Because of liberty about which no one understands anything. We were not ready to give up the liberty of the individual until the liberty of everyone had been obtained.

GENEVIEVE: Didn't we want not to soil our hands with blood?

LANGEVIN: Yes, but in this conflict there are only the hands that are soiled and those which are cut off.

Evidently, it is a question of nothing less than instituting, at whatever the cost, the reign of liberty which the members of the Commune, in the euphoria of an ephemeral victory, had envisioned. It was to be a reign of the abundance which had finally been acquired and parceled out and which is illuminated in a few brief moments by the moving scene in which the people of Paris, pulling out all the stops before the time is ripe for it, consume the goods which do not yet belong to them, but to which they have laid rightful claim.

When he was writing *The Days of the Commune,* Brecht had just joined the young DDR, whose inextricable difficulties strongly resembled those of revolutionary Paris in 1871. There was the same isolation and the same inexperience. Now, at the exact moment that the Stalinist system was becoming extremely militant, Brecht was indicating with sure instinct the paths toward a democratic socialism, predicting well beforehand the changes to be initiated by the Twentieth Congress.

"Expect no more from the Commune than from yourselves." When the school teacher Genevieve takes possession of her ministry, she runs into the passive resistance of the porter, and she doesn't know where the schools are located, or who the teachers are, or who controls their salaries. There is not even any oil in her lamp. She must begin everything again at the beginning and everything at once. To which her friend Langevin answers:

LANGEVIN: The worst of it is that the bureaucrats are concerned with making themselves irreplaceable. That's the way it has been for centuries. But we must find people capable of organizing their work in such a way that they may be replaced at any time. The people who can simplify work are the workers of the future.

This "worker of the future" will no longer be shut off from life and alienated by his function. He will have this *distance* from his work which Brecht is quick to recognize as the source of all pleasure and of an ease which he calls "divine."

It is evident that Brecht does not evade any of the problems which confront a social society in a real, concrete way. But far from confining himself to the immediate present, he always resolves them in the context of the future. While careful of the means, he never forgets the end. To those who, in West Germany, were to reproach him for low compromises, Brecht opposes this positive answer:

LANGEVIN: Citizens, let us not pretend to be infallible as all the governments of the world have done up till now. Our actions ought to be public. Let us interest the masses in our errors. We have nothing to fear but ourselves.

These masses, so long mute and passive, are now seen thinking, fighting, but also loving. They are making their way from a vulgarly materialistic conception of love toward more delicate and also richer forms. Only at the expense of a common battle do men and women in Brecht's work overcome their private conflicts. The following brief dialogue will be often quoted, but we must be careful, however, not to give it a mystical interpretation. It must be situated in its context, that of barricades and a hopeless conflict:

JEAN: We know nothing.
GENEVIEVE: Right now, Jean, we are learning.
JEAN: When we're rolling in the dust, that will be of great help to us.
GENEVIEVE: That will be of great help to us, Jean.
JEAN: What good is it to us, to you and me, to know since we are going to die?
GENEVIEVE: I wasn't talking about *you* and *me*; I said *us*. "We" is much more than "you and I."
JEAN: I only hope that there will be enough of us with us.
GENEVIEVE: The right belongs to everybody.

Now we are going to examine two plays which, although written one at the beginning of the war and the other at the end of the war, are both inspired by the Chinese theater. In *The Good Woman of Setzuan* (1938–1939), Brecht again takes up a problem which he had begun to ponder in his first works: How far does man's liberty extend? This time he chooses a borderline case, that of extreme misery. His Setzuan, less imaginary than one would believe, is really an inferno. There famine is so great that man is reduced to suicide or murder. Are these alternatives unavoidable? "The province of Setzuan," says Brecht in making the point clearer, "is the symbol of all the places where man is exploited by other men. Today it is no longer one of them." So this hell is not at all metaphysical. With all this taken into account, can it be penetrated by grace? No, since three gods, having descended from a heaven, an abstract nothing, pay it a visit, looking for the one just man who, in their opinion, would suffice to justify the hell. And as they find this man in the person of a young prostitute, they give her a chance. They offer her a little tobacco store so that she may live honorably. Will she be able to make the most of this hope-filled chance which is at once so insignificant and so immense?

"I hope," says Shen Te, "that now I shall be able to do much good."

For Shen Te, wealth is then more than a goal: it is an instrument of liberation. She would like to "elevate herself," but in the moral sense of the word. She harbors no avarice in her: is not possession the prerequisite to giving, and even to giving of oneself? Yes, but reality demands a more precise accounting. Who is giving what to whom? From whom did the gods take this tobacco shop that they have given to Shen Te? From a poor widow and her numerous children. So this capital of kindness is poisoned. But more important, it is insufficient. The miserable swoop down on Shen Te like a swarm of flies.

> The little ship of salvation
> is on the verge of going under
> for too many people who are drowning
> avidly cling to it.

In brief, to help the others Shen Te must destroy herself. She must become hard and invent a cousin, Shui Ta, a cold, calculating man whom she is to charge with her defense against her own kindness. But the moment she dons the mask of Shui Ta, she assumes his personality as well. Shui Ta delivers the poor over to the police, the poor with whom only yesterday Shen Te had shared her heart. In this system, does wealth really give liberty?

SHUI TA: I place my only hope in the fact that the workers in the cement factory must smoke a lot, for their work, so it is said, wears them out. But it's true that they don't earn very much.

And yet, Shen Te survives under the mask of Shui Ta. She loves the unemployed worker Sun. He is rather an aviator, but what is an aviator who is not flying? He takes advantage of the one who loves him in order to get into flight even if it breaks her heart. Love destroys the one who loves, and yet it is his only chance for freedom. Just the meeting of two solitudes and two miseries makes the world begin to brighten. During this moment of grace, all the barriers that men set up against and between each other already seem less absolute and necessary. And Shen Te, walking in the city before dawn, again finds this happy harmony that the poets have eulogized.

SHEN TE: Returning from the quarter where Sun has his room, I made a great detour. With each step, I was becoming more joyous. I saw the paper boys and the men watering down the streets and the ox-drawn carts loaded with vegetables. People have always told me that when you are in love you walk in the clouds, but what is really beautiful is to walk on the ground, on the asphalt. I tell you, you miss many things if you are not in love or if you don't see the city when it is sitting up in bed just like, or so the poets say, an old worker who inhales great gulps of fresh morning air before picking up his tools. . . .

In this system, some are thirsty and the others cannot sell their water, but for all of them, love is like the fragile promise of another world. Shen Te loves her aviator not for what he is, but for what he could be: "Am I strong enough to awaken all the good that is in him?" But what is good for an aviator? The plane that gives him a chance to fly is his own "good." So in order to fly, Sun will rob Shen Te. Wouldn't it seem that something in this system is false? In it man cannot give fully of himself. He is maltreated because he is badly utilized. An example is Shen Te. Her crusade fails; she is "too good for this world"—this world that could not take full advantage of her kindness. The scandal of it all is this waste of productive energies.

> To get a mouthful of bread
> more roughness is needed
> than to set up an empire.

Is this situation without hope or remedy? No, since a single act of love is enough to bridge the gap between the aviator and those who remain nailed to the ground. Shen Te resolves the antinomy posed ten years earlier in the *Didactic Play for Baden-Baden*. On a rainy day she buys a glass of water, water more precious than that which falls from the sky, from the unemployed Wang and gives it to the unemployed Sun, the aviator who has conquered the same sky.

SHEN TE: I need your water, Wang,
The water you have carried a long time,
The water which tires you out,
I am giving it to this gentleman over here.
He is an aviator. An aviator
Is hardier than other men.
In the society of clouds,
Braving the storms,
He crosses the sky, carrying
Friendly letters
To faraway friends.

It is a gratuitous act, but is it too costly? No, for it reconciles men. It gives a meaning to their work, founds an economy of love, and clarifies the profound ramifications of commerce and exchange. For he who loves a glass of water is more than a glass of water and an aviator's record is more than just the record. Our acts are justified only if they found a human exchange, an exchange that the system disparages, obstructs, and alienates. Immense is the call that man sends out to other men through the misery and murder.

SHEN TE: Those who have the least give the most willingly. Perhaps it is because man loves to show off what he knows how to do. And how could he better show it than in being likable? Meanness is basically nothing more than awkwardness. When a man sings, or builds a machine, or plants rice, it is nothing more than friendship.

Brecht has just defined "gentleness," this timid, unnoticed, everyday form of kindness. It is hidden in our most humble acts each time that we work for others. It is agreeable, it is natural. It introduces a great gust of fresh air into Brecht's universe of necessity. Did he learn this in exile? One thing is certain: Brecht had discovered something beyond distrust. It is not that he demands of man, in the manner of our naïve gods, absolute virtues. But he knows that kindness, although in conflict with the world, exists, that it has the force of an instinct, and that it is contrary to effort and forced expression:

I nailed a Japanese sculpture to the wall,
the mask of a wicked demon, lacquered with gold.

> With compassion I see
> the swollen veins of his forehead, proving
> the effort it takes to be wicked.

Love, if it is the promise of a better world, is as yet no more than a promise. Shen Te is expecting Sun's child, and it is as if the Annunciation were being reenacted once more, as if each newborn child were a Christ to whom the world and its wealth were promised.

SHEN TE: O joy! A little man is forming within my flesh. You can see nothing yet, but he is there; the world awaits him in secret. In the cities people are saying: there's someone to be reckoned with. An aviator!

> Salute this new conqueror
> of unknown mountains, of unattainable countries.
> He carries the mail from man to man
> across the trackless wastes!

But for this child to live, Shen Te (or rather Shui Ta) will have to tread heavily, exploiting other children. The gospel is converted into murder, and love into solitude. Yesterday's lovers have become cynical, cold, unpitying associates. At the hour of judgment, Shen Te accuses the gods.

> In ordering me
> to be good and yet to live
> you have cleft me in two parts
> like so much forked lightning.
> Something in your world
> is false.

But the gods shrug off this attack, for their optimism is boundless: "Be good and all will go well." There is no common measure nor even any common language between men and gods. And yet we unceasingly project into the abstract infinity of heaven our possibilities, our future, and our human chances. Sometimes we rise up in revolt against the gods; but we always return to place our indefatigable faith in them again. Thus we nourish the gods with the best of ourselves: our power to change the world. Now nothing can come to man's aid except man. The time must arrive when, the gods having deserted us, our "religious" need for kindness will become more rigorous than ever. The reason is that these Brechtian gods are also the reincarnation of our consciences which are not-yet-human. They give us no rest, ceaselessly reminding us that the real is not *all* that is possible. They judge from above. They are the voice of our liberty, for man is *in* the world, the world need not crush man. Man can act on the world; it is a *common* power which permits him to surpass, at the same time, the pessimism of Shen Te (I cannot remain in this world) and the optimism of the gods (you must be good). If Brecht, in *The Good Woman of Setzuan* is momentarily moved by grace—this powerful desire in man for concord—he knows that this grace, lived by those who love and almost immediately on the verge of vanishing into obscurity, must bear fruit. In the final analysis, the liberation of man depends on justice. It implies a methodical battle and that is why *The Caucasian Chalk Circle* (1944–1945), which, with *The Life of Galileo*, forms Brecht's testament, defines morality in terms of law.

This play, inspired by an ancient Chinese morality play,[5] again takes up the quasi-universal theme of the judgment of Solomon. Brecht opposes the myth from the very beginning to the moral demands of a modern world. Two collective farms are arguing over some land. One, which specializes in raising sheep, had to abandon it under the pressure of the German advance. The other, a partisan of modern techniques, defended it clandestinely and even developed an irrigation plan in the very midst of combat. But this plan is workable only if it includes the piece of land in question. How are they going to resolve this point of law? A concrete discussion brings about the solution. The agreement is sealed with a feast. The collective farm "Rosa Luxemburg" offers its guests an old popular play that is not without relevance in the present.

This scene can be compared to certain rather rare poems in

5 Li Hsing Tao's play had already been adapted in 1925 by Klabund. A detailed examination, impossible here, would reveal that Brecht had studied this version and that his is, at the beginning at least, no more than a critique of the other.

which Brecht pays tribute to the young Soviet Union. We shall immediately dismiss "Die Erziehung der Hirse" (1951), a fastidious, Mitchurinian epic which gives way in a completely exceptional manner to Stalinist phraseology. On the other hand, we shall retain "The Inauguration of the Moscow Subway" and "The Rugweavers of Kujan-Bulak," both written during the thirties. In the first of these ballads in a new style, the masses are seen taking possession of the goods which they have produced. They are unreasonable; they consume just as they produce: in full possession of the facts. This is a spontaneous, everyday example of what Brecht understands by theater: a critical pleasure. This pleasure can attain its fullness if the world comes back to those who transform it. And that brings into question that concord or harmony which nourishes all lyric sentiment. Brecht integrates it into the very act of transforming things. The weavers of Kujan-Bulak would like to honor the great Lenin. They are poor and shaken by yellow fever. Rather than erect a plaster statue to him, they therefore prefer to buy the oil which will disinfect their village.

"Thus they did themselves a service in honoring Lenin, and they honored him in doing themselves a service, showing in that way that they had understood him."

Having accomplished this act of useful luxury, they decide to record, on a commemorative plaque, the whys and wherefores of their act. It is a *poetic* act or work insofar as it creates not only a material good but also a new *value*. Our weavers tame a hostile environment just as the poet conquers through words a reality that had been reputed up to that time to be prosaic. And doubtless, Brecht could not ask for a more precious honor than that of drafting, for this most human community, a plaque which sanctions an exemplary decision for all.

This new system, which is getting ready to liquidate, even through its conflicts, the bloody divisions of the past, is discovered by Brecht with an emotion that is all the more lively because he had ceaselessly appealed to it as a sort of liberating beyond. For all that, he does not forget what long-suffering patience—or rather impatience—was necessary to establish it.

Grusche, the humble and heroic servant in *The Caucasian Chalk Circle*, becomes the symbol of all those who, in a world of violence, obstinately pursue a work of peace. And if, for once, it gains the upper hand, this is because there has always been a slight chance for the exception. The feudal underlings of Grusinie have risen against the grand duke and his governors because his warlike plans have failed. In all this—and Brecht clearly indicates this—there is a reactionary process, but, for the people, it is also a chance. They profit from it by establishing a very provisionary anarchy. If they were not tempted, through ignorance, to attribute the events to the influence of the comets, they would found their regime well before its time. But the time was not ripe. And yet in the midst of this universal upheaval, Grusche succeeds in instituting a new rule, that of liberty. And here is her story:

During a palace revolution, the wife of a governor, occupied above all with her clothes and jewels, abandons her newborn child. This lack of conscience, which is much worse than natural badness, betrays the alienation of the rich. It is an alienation in objects that Grusche, since she possesses nothing, could not share. She hears a cry of distress, and we find her in the throes of what Brecht calls "the terrible temptation of kindness." And yet Grusche hesitates throughout the night before adopting the child. Her fiancé is waiting for her; she knows that kindness in this world is too heavy a burden, and that is why she continues to hope until dawn that someone will come to take the foundling off her hands.

Grusche's hesitation is realistic because kindness, to be effective, must be allied to ruse. The affection of a mother for her child is not given; it is cultivated. Work establishes emotional relationships; the effort expended to ameliorate something makes it dear and indispensable, and that is why the rich woman cannot really love her son. Grusche's acts of love are, each time, the fruit of a tragic conflict. A passage in *The Dialectic in the Theater*, taken live from a panel discussion at the Berliner Ensemble, develops this idea:

R.: I find this hesitation of Grusche very beautiful. Kindness is limited. In each being there is just so much kindness, no more, no less. It also depends on circumstances. It can be consumed, it can be reestablished, etc.

w.: It is a realistic conception.

BRECHT: I find it too mechanical, not kind enough. Why not instead say this: Bad times make kindness a danger for the good. In the servant Grusche, there is the interest for the child and the interest for herself, and both are in conflict. She must differentiate between the two interests, recognize them, and make an effort to satisfy both of them at once.

Grusche's battle against "the terrible temptation of kindness" ends in defeat, but it is a happy defeat. Brecht, whose optimism can be surprising, leads us to believe that her choice cannot go without being repaid since it is just and in accord with the real sense of life.

As she was hesitating on the doorstep, she
heard, or thought she heard, a feeble call. The child was crying,
He was not trembling, no: he was crying out these intelligible words,
at least she thought she heard him say: Woman, come to my aid.
And pursuing his appeal, in intelligible words, he also said,
"May you know, woman, that he who does not wish to hear
a call for help, he who passes, blocking his ears,
he will never more hear the tender call of the lover
nor the blackbird just before dawn, nor the happy sigh of
the tired vineyard keeper at the hour of the Angelus . . ."

The poetic sentiment that Brecht instills in Grusche is in no way usurped. It is the reward for an irreproachable conscience. What the poets have eulogized appears here purified and delivered out of all illusory intoxication. For beauty is not in things, but in a peaceful heart. What establishes lyric harmony for Brecht is moral harmony between oneself and others. This harmony, however, is not an absence of conflict: Grusche, in order to maintain it, will have to make up her mind to kill. But in killing a soldier who wanted to snatch the child from her, she defends a possession which belongs to her and which, at the same time, does not belong to her. Her act then, which is so serious, will be justified only if the child becomes entirely and definitively hers. Then only will this act be *her* act, serving, like those of her class, the human future. Hence, we see the necessity of a quasi-holy appropriation. At the foot of the Janga-Tau glacier, at the moment when she must face the abyss with her precious burden, Grusche really adopts her child. She changes his clothes and baptizes him symbolically. From this time forward, the child is becoming a new man: he has changed classes. He passes from his condition at birth to a so-to-speak supernatural condition. This passage founds a new legal right which is no longer that of blood. It establishes holy bonds between a mother and her child. And so it is that in this new system of relationships the goods of this world will be called upon to change hands. In this system he who takes possession of things becomes the owner of them. It is curious that Brecht, in order to sanction this reversal, has very conscious recourse to religious symbols whose origin is lost in the night of time.

All transformation of society is accompanied by an obscure mutation of consciences. Our most common speech betrays signs of this.

AZDAK: At Tiflis, they hanged a landlord, a Turk. He could prove to them that he had quartered his servants as the custom decreed and not cut them in two. His zeal was above all suspicion. In spite of that they hanged him like a brigand, simply because he was a Turk. He could do nothing about it, right? So he ended up on the gibbet like Pontius Pilate in the Creed.

This is not the first time that one of Brecht's characters has brought up this detail about the Creed. Very unusual indeed. The only historical allusion among all these metaphysical formulations concerns a judge. It accuses him of the murder of an innocent man. He did not kill him, but neither did he defend him. It is a passive guilt through omission. This verdict marks a new stage in the juridical conscience. Henceforth, he who accepts an injustice will be no less guilty than he who commits it. It is to this audacious paradox that Brecht's popular characters willingly have recourse when an irregularity obscures a more profound rule. The rich man in the example of Azdak has been condemned because he is a Turk. This injustice (in terms of the justice of the rich) is seen as converted, however, into a possible justice. He could have, or should have, been condemned not as a Turk, but as an imperialist. Thus what is unjust in the eyes of one class becomes just in the eyes of another. And so in one fell swoop we have an illustration of the relativity of all jurisprudence.

Justice for Brecht is not an absolute, but a social fact. The judge founds the law. He derives his worth only from the interests that he represents. "The judgment of the robe of a judge would have more weight than that of a judge without a robe." A perfect justice then would be the one which would represent the interest of a classless society. At this extreme the conscience of each person would be his own judge and every mistake would carry the implication of its punishment in itself. But things are far from settled. For the time being, Azdak, the extravagant, drunken vagrant proclaims only a justice of the class. His judgments are only an approximation of real justice. They are imperfect, and that is why they themselves ought to be judged.

The second part of *The Caucasian Chalk Circle* is to some extent the trial of a judge. There, cunning and cowardice are brought out into broad daylight. The absurdity of his judgments comes into accord with reason in an unexpected way, but only because, for once, the poor are being judged by a poor man. The wife of the governor and Grusche are arguing over the child. Azdak knows very well that both of them are lying, but that isn't the problem: it is a question of affirming a new truth. One invokes the bonds of the blood, the other those of work. To clear it up, Azdak gives them the test of Solomon. The result, however, is different from that in the Old Testament. It is Grusche who will give in, thus proving that she deserves the child.

> Things ought to go to those who are good to them.
> Thus: children to maternal women in order that they prosper,
> cars to good drivers in order that they may be well driven,
> and the valley to those who irrigate it, so that it may produce fruit.

But in order for this verdict to become effective, Grusche must adhere to it, must question not only the judge but also justice itself. She is faced with the ultimate temptation at the instant when Azdak asks her if she would not like to see her child rich and powerful. In refusing to fall for the trap that the system has set for her, she chooses *her* class and the values of her class. By doing this, she approves and prepares a new relationship between man and man, between men and things.

The story has a happy ending. Grusche finds the man she loves: "I kept this child because that Sunday we had become engaged. Thus he has become a child of love." You would say that, finally free, Grusche's heart begins to sing. Up to that point she was the voice of Brecht. When her emotion became too lively, she would become speechless, and it would devolve upon the old cantor Avkadi Tcheidse to describe the movements of her heart. These lyric commentaries are in no way aimed at emotion. And yet they are moving. With precision they weigh the motives of the slightest gesture. But since no one can judge himself, another must plead for Grusche. "The smallest social unity," says Brecht, "is not a man, but *two* men." The same thing applies to the language of the interior life.

9 · Concerning a Nonheroic Ethic
Kalendergeschichten · The Business Deals of
Mr. Julius Caesar · The Life of Galileo

> I believe only in witnesses who wouldn't cut
> each other's throats.
>
> JEAN ROSTAND

WE KNOW very little about Brecht's private life. It seems, nevertheless, that he tried to subject it to some rules of conduct.
These rules are set down in the *Stories of Mr. Keuner*, a series of
aphorisms which he had been developing and elaborating upon
since 1930 and collected in a sort of popular almanac, the
Kalendergeschichten (1948). Keuner is Brecht's ironical brother.
Here the portrait tends toward caricature. Brecht considers himself a foreigner, and if he consents to taking us partially into his
confidence, he still shows himself to us as he would like to be.
His Keuner is, to some extent, a Mr. Teste [1] of practical reason.
He intends to establish a correct relationship with his surroundings. His taste for nature is moderated. Whoever takes advantage
of it, whoever enjoys it without working at it, becomes, according to Brecht, infected by an unhealthy fever. And yet it happens that K. is tired of a civilization where nothing exists except
in function of its utility. The vision of a tree comforts him.
The tree is not only useful, it is also likable. This is the necessary
part of gratuitousness, of nondependence (etwas beruhigend
Selbstständiges, von mir Absehendes), that the carpenter himself ought to recognize and respect. For a civilization which
cannot answer the question "Why eat?" is not one. Man cannot go without friendship; it is a necessary luxury. K., however,

1 The titular character of a novel by Paul Valéry.

is not willing to admit that it goes as far as sacrifice. A person can come to the aid of another without doing damage to himself. It is a question of economy and intelligence. K. detests brilliant but useless discussions. He searches out the company of men who approach their neighbors as the worker approaches nature: with the end in view of transforming them. K. sloughs off all unproductive friendship. But if he makes a break, he is always careful to explain the break. Every question is worth an answer: his behavior toward others, even if it is negative, ought to be of some profit to him. "Whoever offends reason," says Mr. K., "offends me." And that is why his love has no meaning unless it improves that which he loves.

The utilization of reason, however, is difficult. Whoever would clarify human relationships runs into the obscurity of the times. In the last resort, it is a political problem. Is there a common rule for reasonable people? Yes, according to K.; it is the fidelity to contracts. But just the same, changing situations would seem to make them useless. This answer can take one by surprise, and K. himself contradicts it. If he declares that the Party is right when it condemns those who are forced to betray the Party by the Party itself, he also affirms that even this Party "could not be expected to have an answer to everything." The reason is that K., according to Brecht, is anything but simple. Searching for truth, he avoids the most pressing one of all: "Someone asked Mr. K. if a god existed. Mr. K. answered: I advise you to consider whether your behavior would be modified by my answer. If not, then we can drop the subject. If yes, then I can tell you that you have already decided: you need a god."

Brecht takes up this theme again in a poem called "The Parable of Buddha." To disciples who keep pressing him with questions concerning nirvana, the master answers that they resemble a man who would hesitate to go out of a house in flames. It is certainly not by chance that Brecht describes dialectical materialism as proceeding from Buddhist nihilism. This is even in accord with the interior movement of his mental processes. Besides, the two ways of thinking give in to a single despair before that-which-is. But while the Buddha (like the young Brecht) takes refuge in the absence of desires and the sleep of the unconscious, Marxism (and, consequently, the Brecht of the thirties) works toward a revolutionary refusal (*nichtdulden*), a transformation about whose outcome (and this point must be insisted upon) Brecht is none too clear. The immediate danger counts here, whether it is a question of a fire or of "the growing numbers of bombers in a capitalist sky." Of course, it is true that Buddha reserves an ulterior response. He claims a stay of proceedings. His I-do-not-know resembles, and yet does not resemble, that of Socrates: it implies a "but-I-shall-try-to-know" as well.

It is evident that Brecht in no way denies the obscurity, but he refuses to obscure it still further under the pretext of clarifying it. Another poem, "The Shoe of Empedocles," shows clearly how he rejects metaphysics. In it Brecht tackles the enigma of death, taking and criticizing a theme which Hölderlin had set up as a myth, assimilating the suicide of Empedocles in the sacrifice of Christ. The Brechtian Empedocles also intends to give a meaning to death. But more than that, he chooses *his* death, wishing to escape the weariness of age. Nevertheless, it is not through pride, for far from breaking with the others, he discreetly goes away, withdrawing from those around him, letting his face blend in with all those who have preceded him to the grave. His disciples even need some time to notice his absence. But we see them questioning each other on the shoe that Etna has spewed forth. Couldn't that be construed as the ultimate ruse of the philosopher? Once again, he wishes to give something over which to ponder. He dies to educate and his unusual death suddenly brings the meaning of his teaching to light. It could be said that for Brecht death *alienates* existence, clarifying all that it possesses which is unique, strange and, therefore, instructive. He is setting up an exception, but here the exception leads us to the rule. There is nothing miraculous about Empedocles's shoe. It is "tangible, worn, and earthly," the symbol of this new religion which reduces man to his moral condition and deprives him of all metaphysical hope. Can one even speak, in this case, of a symbol? This shoe is not the visible sign of an invisible reality; it is not situated at the crossroads of two orders. Let us say more simply that it is a testament "left for all those who, from the moment when they no longer see, begin to believe."

This concern for demystification is evident throughout the *Kalendergeschichten*. There Brecht reduces various heroes of history to the common denominator. However, it would be wrong to believe that he is aiming for some sort of abstract leveling. He admits the exceptional being on the condition that he be in proper relation to the masses. Three novellas in the *Kalendergeschichten* define this relation. One of them recounts the old age of Bacon, a bad judge, but a good scholar. Not having succeeded in dominating men, he makes an effort to help them dominate nature. Although his effulgence is discreet, it is immense. It is manifested, on the most everyday level, in his relationships with the young groom Dick. A little scientific experiment, which Bacon conducts quite by chance one day on an outing, becomes, for Dick, the great experiment of an entire lifetime. It incites him to imitate the new behavior of his master in the manual domain which is his proper field of action. It teaches him to risk his life to verify a hypothesis, no matter how unimportant, in order to *know*. Bacon is an astonishing educator; he does not try to put himself "on the level of his pupil" (which would be a sign of disdain), but to elevate the pupil's level. Examining with him the words most commonly used, he initiates Dick to the ethics of a new era. For example, Bacon interests him in constantly verifying the usage which he makes of the word "good." You can say that bread is good, for it is good for the man. But when Dick's superstitious grandmother asserts that Bacon is bad, she is unconsciously mixed up in metaphysics. Since every man is good and bad at the same time, the question is rather to know *in what* and *for whom* he is good or bad. Only in their social consequences can one judge acts.

Brecht also illustrates the famous "valet's point of view." It is an effective criterion. The value of truly great men is in no way diminished by it. Rather, it is in minor, forgotten episodes that their action becomes clear and definitive in the eyes of the crowd. In 1949, Brecht published a few fragments of a novel which he entitled, significantly, *The Business Deals of Mr. Julius Caesar*. This was to be an experimental novel which aimed more to instruct than to distract the masses. What do they expect from a novelist? Love fascinates them; for them, it is one of the inexplicable forces of destiny. The novel is supposed to explain it to them. Business, on the contrary, leaves them indifferent. It is excluded from the storytelling realm, for the masses do not realize that it influences their everyday existence as much as love, if not more so. Now Brecht, justly, would like to enlighten them, enhancing their power and, consequently, their liberty. But this power and liberty are still so new that we can scarcely take pleasure in them.

As austere as it may be, this second novel by Brecht is not, however, boring. It stimulates the imagination by unveiling with the ruse of a detective story, what goes on behind the scenes of this official story which justifies the powerful and ignores the weak. History needs heroes, fixes the attention of the masses on them, and distracts these masses from the real motives of the event. Thus Caesar, or rather the Caesarian myth, has unceasingly in the past inspired a long series of reactionary solutions. Brechtian criticism is aimed more at the myth than at the man. It intends to be objective; it is never petty. For heroic history, Brecht substitutes proletarian history. The absence of documents makes this a difficult undertaking; were not the historians always seated at the tables of the great? Their testimony, however, is our only source, and it is up to us to uncover the class interests which could have instigated the events. Brecht maneuvers this reversal with consummate skill. The truth that he gleans from it does not in the least pretend to be absolute. It is *another* truth of another class, the class to which the slave Rarus belonged. It is he whom Brecht charges with observing his master.

This master is disconcerting. Cynical? In part, but he happens to get trapped in his own game. The least that can be said is that he is not frank and open with himself. But indeed are we, and Rarus, himself, is he any more so? We remain outside the conscience of the hero. His social behavior and his explanation of it are the two coordinates of our relative knowledge. In an often subtle manner they are contradictory, but from this contradiction springs truth, a critical truth which unceasingly dissociates Caesar as-he-is-seen from Caesar as-he-would-like-to-be-seen.

The social novel, if it is perceptive of the language and action of the exterior world, ought to make an effort to "situate" its character. It does not refer back to the emotional motives of his behavior, but to the collective dynamisms which determine it. For the "great men" are only puppets in a game which is out of their hands. They are swept along by history rather than being the makers of it. If Caesar, for an instant, succeeds, it is because he had the luck to be in the right place at the right moment. So there we have our hero brought back to the ranks of "workman of history."

Had he no more than a simple plan, some ideas (and he happens to adopt very sincerely those of the democrat Alexander), he would not be able to apply them. Caesar has some debts, and his only intention is to repay them. He does not choose: he is a man with his back to the wall, trapped in the game of supply and demand. Hence, we see alternating depression and nervous exaltation which we have already noticed in the swindlers of *The Threepenny Novel*.

Caesar wishes to wrap himself in a tissue of legend, but Rarus, his slave, knows each thread of this tissue. What is his testimony worth? Rarus is anything but a "privileged conscience." He must also "get himself straightened out" and his expedients are hardly more heroic than those of Caesar. He is a small-time swindler in the wake of a great one. He is a little more than a slave (hence his clairvoyance) and a little less than a free man (hence his dependence). This ambiguous situation is reflected in his judgments. On the decisive (in appearance) day of Cicero's Catiline oration, Rarus, absorbed in his sentimental troubles, can find only one fact to record in his journal: the rain. But this notation, for Brecht, has more weight than all the falsified eloquence of a Cicero.

A novella from the *Kalendergeschichten* enters, furthermore, to complete this fragment of a novel. The interests of Rarus and Caesar at the ultimate hour for settling accounts are separated. The hero, rejected by history, chooses to die and this choice is, perhaps, his only free act. But Rarus does not die *his* own death, but one which is imposed upon him. It is a bad gamble to bet on the powerful. The history of Rarus is, in fact, only prehistoric. For the man of the masses, history will only really begin the day that he acquires his liberty. And this history will be nonheroic.

Brecht amasses all these themes in *The Life of Galileo*, which can be justly considered to be his testament. The autobiographical allusions in it seem to be numerous, and although Brecht conceived it in 1938, it is the last work over which he labored.

In conformity to the rules of his epic theater, of which *Galileo* is the most finished example, the life of the great scientist is split into autonomous scenes. There is no center of gravity, neither is there any dramatic progression. Ascending or descending, Galileo is never the same. He is a contradictory person who, up to the last minute, is hesitating and questioning himself. "The universe," cries out the young Galileo, "has lost its center. One night is enough for it to discover an infinity of them. Each of us has become the center, each of us and yet no one." We have already encountered this assertion in *A Man's a Man*, but there it is colored by pessimism. Here, it expresses the joyful, careless adherence to a new ethic founded on the doubt that Galileo opposes to the congealed hierarchy of feudal values. For him everything is changing, the world and he who observes it. He is discovering space as we, today, are discovering time. To the young Sarti who objects: "But I don't perceive the earth turning," he answers: "Because you are turning with it." For one must put a distance between himself and things in order to understand them; he must exclude himself from them and cut the umbilical cord. It is an adult, scientific approach which is simultaneously accompanied by distress and pleasure.

To combat the system, Galileo needs leisure or, in other words, money. Therein lies his first contradiction. He lays claim to an absolute liberty which the system refuses him. He must then choose between two relative liberties: between Venice, which welcomes scholars but pays them badly, and Florence, which censures their writings but offers them an easy life. Galileo, between these two restrictions, chooses the one which he judges to be the lesser: he decides on the court of Florence. Is he wrong? No, for outside the system he cannot act. He can make use of it, but not escape it. The only liberty which counts in his eyes is the liberty to produce. Poverty paralyzes him. To escape from it, he perpetrates a fraud in passing himself off as the inventor of the telescope. It is true that he makes up for it immediately by discovering an unsuspected use for this stolen instrument. Thus, at the same time that he is yielding to social pressure, Galileo is liberating himself from it. We shall say then, as does Brecht, that his relation to the world is just.

This relation is revolutionary. The Aristotelian philosophers oppose a medieval conception of order to it. In it the earth (relative) is submissive to heaven (the absolute); there man appears as the "crown of creation." Now our philosophers accuse Galileo of wanting to dethrone man. For them, everything revolves about man, while man, in his opinion, revolves around things. But in the same breath that they are proclaiming the royalty of man, the detractors of Galileo are menacing him with physical punishments, thus betraying the faults of their system.

This conflict between two humanisms is taken up again in depth in the discussion which opposes Galileo to a young monk, a natural philosopher, whose sincerity could not, for once, be doubted. This monk is the son of peasants; he has fashioned himself the champion of the miserable, his brethren. Wasn't the old order giving them at least some reasons, even though illusory, for living? He was justifying their misery and conferring upon it the sacred character of the necessary, the immutable. There they are betrayed: "We can only," they say, "count on ourselves. The eye of God abandons us; we open ours and we see that we are ignorant, aging, and completely worn out. Our misery no longer has meaning. Hunger is no longer a test; it is not-having-eaten. Effort is no longer a service; it is drudgery-and-abasement. Nothing more."

Galileo's answer is hard, but it comes from a more demanding love. Misery no longer has meaning. To the aesthetic ethics of the past, Galileo opposes a morality of health and happiness. This pathetic renunciation includes even the notion of genius.

GALILEO: Do you know how the margaritifera oyster produces its pearl? By absorbing a foreign, unbearable body as, for example, a grain of sand which imperils his life. And this process almost destroys it each time. To hell with the pearl; I take the side of the oyster!

Even there, this position-taking is paradoxical. Galileo preaches the rule, the common measure, while he himself is a flagrant exception. He is the man who, at the moment when the plague plunges all Florence into panic and famine, only dreams of obtaining a rare book. Such behavior his landlady judges, with good reason, to be irrational. But doesn't every act of faith imply a certain degree of irrationality? In opposition to his friend Sangredo, who sees only the inertia and the violence of the mobs, Galileo has confidence in man.

SANGREDO: Where is God?
GALILEO: Am I a theologian? I am a mathematician.
SANGREDO: Before all else, you are a man. So I ask where is God in your system?
GALILEO: In us or nowhere.

There is a god in man, and this god is reason. It is the dignity of man that he knows how to convince and let himself be convinced, how to modify his opinions and not resist "the sweet violence of truth." For reason bathes us everywhere; it is inscribed in things. "If nature," says Galileo, "were under the influence of different laws, our brain too would differ." That is to suppose an original harmony between the world and man. It gives Galileo the power to say against all evidence: "They had the entire world against them and they were right." Galileo loves the possibilities of man; Sangredo loves men as they are.

Sangredo is a pessimist, and yet, in his everyday decisions, he is less cynical than Galileo. Galileo sacrifices men and even the happiness of his daughter to this notion of a finally liberated man that he would like to promote. Both are human and necessary, and Brecht accepts them both. And yet it so happens that Galileo frightens him as, in a sense, he frightens himself.

GALILEO: What a terrifying night is the one when man discovers the truth! What an hour of blindness is the one when he takes it upon himself to believe in human reason! Of whom can one say that he is a seer? Of the man who is about to die.

Galileo really has a *passion* for the truth, and he knows that this passion is satanic. He would deprive himself of light to know what the light is. He prefers the knowledge of things to the things themselves. "Like a lover, like a drunkard, like a traitor," he is excluded from paradise. And he who knows cannot help but disseminate his knowledge. His passion is contagious; "it is really a vice which leads to unhappiness." Thence, there is a defiance and an appeal: "How much longer shall I be able to cry out in this furnace? That is the question!"

Here we touch the heart of Brechtian tragedy. Man knows that his curiosity is accursed. And yet this demoniacal instinct for truth is so essential to him that he must obey it, even if he may die because of it. It is apparent that we are quite far from the optimism of a "progressivist" lyricism. Intelligence for Brecht is only a tiny light, storm-tossed on an ocean of shadows. It must not go out. But the effort is disproportionate to the few results. Occasionally, Brecht becomes impatient; he would like to break away from so many uncertainties, but wisdom leads him back to the common measure: "the goal is not to open the doors to an infinite truth, but to impose a limit on infinite measure."

Galileo, like Brecht, has grown older; the insolent arrogance of his youth has disappeared. He sees himself deprived little by little of the worldly harmony which had once duped him, but his humble working companions—his smelter, his glassmaker, his housekeeper—encourage him to live. Their good sense inspires him continually. It is for them that he works, writing no longer in Latin, but in the language of the people. Moreover, his ideas have determined their path: they inspired the carnival of 1632. If the sun stops turning about the earth, why would the pope and the king be the center of the world? A secular hierarchy founders; the stars no longer succeed in justifying the exploitation of men by other men.

Galileo could not have done what he did if he had not been protected and discreetly understood by his landlady, Mrs. Sarti. Here Brecht weaves delicate bonds. In the time of the plague, Mrs. Sarti makes the decision not to follow her children in order not to abandon Galileo, a great child himself. In her humble way, she is revolutionary; her reason is that of the heart, and at the exact moment that she follows her inclinations, her relations with Galileo know a brief period of grace. This is expressed by an ephemeral passage from the formal *you* to the familiar *thou*. Two humans in danger suddenly discover what they owe to each other, what each gives and receives, and what links them together above and beyond social conventions. And like all grace, this manifestation is easy and natural.

Galileo's ethics are complex and vary according to his age. At fifty years, they are intransigent: "I tell you: whoever ignores the truth is an imbecile. But he who knows it and conceals it is an assassin." Ten years later they are softened and full of nuances. Galileo is, basically, a man of the flesh. "He thinks," says one of his disciples, "as he enjoys. He could no more refuse a new idea than a glass of good wine." If he takes deadly risks, it is because science is a stronger instinct in him than the instinct for self-preservation. When the attrition of old age unexpectedly arrives, intelligence is degraded and nothing remains but the elementary instincts.

Is Galileo still himself at the moment when he renounces himself? Yes and no. Yes, in his constant concern for taking instruction from even his failings. He pretends in no way to justify these failings. One day he will admit that if he were to recant, it would in no way be through ruse, but through fear of suffering. Never was Galileo more human than in this moment of admission. Through it, he shows himself to be many centuries ahead of his contemporaries. Even in his weakness, he is founding a new, realistic moral code. There is no absolute morality, only the morality of the lesser evil. "As regards obstacles," says Galileo, "the shortest distance between two points can be a curve."

This relativistic morality is scarcely understood by Galileo's disciples. In their eyes the test to which the Inquisition subjected Galileo poses a heroic dilemma. Will violence carry the day over intellect? They would have this intellect all-powerful; they are of the persuasion that Galileo will resist.

> ANDREA: No, violence is not enough. Madness has been conquered; it is not invulnerable. No, man does not fear death.
> DEDERZONI: If not, it would be as if, the day hardly dawning, night were to redescend.
> ANDREA: But today everything has changed. Man raises his head and the oppressed cry out: I can live! Everything will be won if only someone gets up and says *no*.

Galileo rejects this individualistic morality in a single sentence: "Unhappy is the country that needs a hero!" It is precisely because one alone is not enough. We give too much importance to the hero; we expect too much from him. The disciples have sacrificed everything to science and now the master is renouncing it "being concerned only with saving his guts." We share their feeling of revolt, but we also admire the courage and serenity of Galileo. At this time he is gauging the limits of his liberty. It is no longer the time when the salvation of all depends on the sacrifice of one. All men depend on all other men to varying degrees. Alone, Galileo can do nothing. Yes, he is afraid of death; yes, violence finally triumphs over the intellect. But what is true for the individual is not for the species. For it converts the fear and weakness of many into courage and force.

A prisoner of the Inquisition, spied upon by his daughter, constantly watched, Galileo, a greedy, blind old man has only one ultimate concern: to transfer one last manuscript to his disciple Andrea so that he can get it into Holland. The story does not end with the death of the hero. He can very well accuse himself of having "betrayed science," but he could not set himself up as judge of his own existence. He has recognized his limits, but in recognizing them, he has surpassed himself. It is history that judges him.

Thus, the anguish of youth is converted into a serene confidence. The exiled Brecht (and who is to say that his last years too were not an exile?) continues, against all reason, instructing his son, watering trees, and writing poems. Is it the hope of despair?

Today, Easter Sunday, at dawn
a snowstorm struck the island.
Between the clumps of trees which were already getting green
there was snow. My young son
led me toward a little apricot tree very close to the house,
dragging me away from a line in which I was denouncing with
  a vengeful finger
those who prepare a war which
risks wiping out the continent, this island, my people,
my family and myself. Quietly
we covered the frozen bush
with a sack.

In a time hostile to the intellect, Brecht pursued "at any cost" the politics of the intellect. You can see irony in his situation. Performed in the West, ignored in the East, and badly understood everywhere, he left us a work which already begins to live with its own life. Officialdom everywhere makes use of it in whatever way convenient, but we know what Brecht thought of officialdom. "In 1948," a witness reports, "The Cultural Association for the Democratic Renovation of Germany had organized a reception in honor of the writer in East Berlin. Brecht was seated between Wilhelm Pieck and the Soviet political advisor, Colonel Toulpanov. Someone had just given a very pathetic and absolutely anti-Brechtian speech. Then Brecht arose. His birdlike head slightly forward, he glanced at the assembly, shook hands with Pieck and then with Toulpanov, then sat down and began on his soup. A long minute had passed before the table conversations managed to get started again."

Domestic Sermons · One Hundred Poems ·
Poems of Exile · Buchow Elegies

> And in times of obscurity
> Can we sing then too?
> We shall sing just the same,
> We shall sing the obscurity of the times . . .

POETRY is also—and above all—a pleasure. This pleasure can be
born only from a sentiment of harmony. But how can we sing
of harmony in a time of discord? The *Domestic Sermons*, which
Brecht published in 1927, shows that he was haunted by the
imminence of catastrophe. Nature, far from offering the poet
a refuge, sets a trap for him. Hostile, convulsive, strange, inexplicable, it lays open terrifying chasms beneath the asphalt
streets of the cities. The city itself is a jungle. The trees that are
chopped down there grow back ever more thickly and rapidly.
Whoever sleeps becomes swallowed up by it; why resist? Since
nature always has the last word, let us give up our identity and
espouse decay. And so it is that the young Brecht comes to
dream of an impossible alliance. He invites us to rejoin the tops
of the trees, from where a person moves (or thinks he moves)
everything. Brecht was soon to discover the vanity of this
gratuitous falsehood.

In 1926 a German review organized a literary contest. It
charged Brecht with judging some four hundred entries by
young poets. All of them took pleasure in that evanescent
lyricism for which Rilke, their predecessor, had given them
their taste. An irritated Brecht denounced them all as "delicate
dreamers and sentimental spokesmen of a winded bourgeoisie,"
and proposed, not without humor, to award the prize to a
robust and naïve poem which had appeared in a sporting sheet

in honor of a champion bicyclist. This defiance must be taken
into consideration. What this means is that Brecht now realizes
that poetry, if it can no longer respond to some social demand,
is doomed to disappear. Why would the poet Brecht write since
no one any longer knows what a poem is, since no one reads
them or pays for them? The question is posed in a poem written
during the thirties, but if Brecht announces that he is going on
strike, it is to turn immediately toward a public which poetry
had neglected up to that point. For centuries it had been addressed to the privileged classes. Privilege itself "dosing out
words like drugs, keeping only the strongest and the best,"
offered these classes something like an extra possession:

> All that you enjoy we eulogize
> So that you can enjoy it once more: the flesh of
> Our women, the sadness of autumn and the
> Stream sliding by in the light of the moon . . .

Ten years later, depicting a plunderer perched in his cherry
tree, Brecht sings, in familiar terms, of the joy of offering the
fruits of his labor. This poem institutes a new form of poetic
possession. There, the song is born of a just harmony between
the act of consuming and that of producing. However, this
harmony is the fruit of a long critical effort. First of all it is
self-criticism, for everything leads one to think that, in other
times, Brecht would have inclined to a more intimate lyricism,
exempt from soul-rending conflicts. A poem of youth, one of
his rare amorous confidences, would suffice to prove that. What
remains after an instant of grace is not the person loved (he is
transformed) nor his memory (it dies), but such clouds as
were passing over the lovers, such detail, gratuitous in appearance, which surpasses their love and which only the poem retains. The secrets of poetry could not be used with more delicate
ease. Brecht converts these secrets and this technique over to
ends which have been wrongfully reputed to be nonpoetic. In
an essay on "Unrhymed Poetry in Irregular Verse" (1939), he
remarks that "our acoustical surroundings have been prodigiously
modified." Any poet who intends to discipline poetry ought to
renounce, henceforward, the continuity of traditional verse and

take his inspiration from the broken, demonstrative rhythms, taking his example from street hawkers, news vendors, and processions of workers. Quoting Luther, that great artisan of the German language, Brecht demands that a sentence obey what he calls a *gestus*, or in other words, a concern for an active communication. Thus, Luther does not write: "Pluck out the eye that hurts you!" but, modifying the original text, he translates: "If your eye hurts you, pluck it out!" "You can see right off," concludes Brecht, "that this formation is richer and purer." The beginning of the sentence expresses a postulate. Its intonation is just, for it expresses the unusual, exceptional character of it. Then, after an instant's pause or indecision, the advice descends like the blade of a guillotine, unexpected and scandalous.

Brechtian prosody is subject to discussion. The best of translations gives no more than an imperfect image of this. Nevertheless, I would like to show what rigor and reflection accompany, in Brecht's poetry, the abandon of traditional versification.

> Here, in this shroud of zinc
> Lies a dead man
> Or else his legs and his head,
> Or still less of what he was
> Or nothing since he was
> An agitator.
>
> He has been identified as the cause of all evils.
> Stick him in the ground. It is better
> That only his wife go with him to the carrion pit,
> For he who accompanies him,
> He too will be a marked man.
>
> That thing there in the zinc
> Has excited you to great misdeeds:
> To eat in your hunger and
> To dress warmly and
> To feed your children and
> To demand your due and
> To the solidarity with all
>
> The oppressed, your brethren, and
> To think.

And that thing there in the zinc has said
That there must be another system of production,
And that you, the massed millions of working men,
Must assume its direction.
Until then, the future will hold nothing better for you.

And because that thing there in the zinc has said these words,
It has been put in zinc and must be buried in secret,
As an agitator for having aroused you.
And all those who will speak of eating their fill
And all those among you who will want to dress warmly
And all those among you who will demand their due
And all those who will want to nourish their children
And all those who will think and declare their solidarity
With all those who are opposed,
Henceforward and forever they will end up in zinc
Just like that one there, like the agitators
Who must be buried in secret.

The motive of the discourse is not, as with an Eluard,[1] a connected sequence of images. Far from casting a spell, the effects of repetition (and . . . and . . . and) alert the attention, create an uneasiness and a questioning. The rhythm is no longer mechanical in any way. It is wedded to the processes of active thought, engaged in an effort to know. This effort is all the more arduous because it is up against the wear and tear of everyday speech. Now if Brecht wants to use the most neutral words, he finds himself constrained to alienate or unsettle them in order to give them back their freshness and power to move. The current formula would be, for example: "Er hat euch verhetzt, eure Kinder zu füttern": He excited you to nourish your children. But Brecht writes: "Er hat euch verhetzt zum Die Kinder füttern," which literally means: "to the feeding-of-children." His intention is evident. To feed the children is, for the man of the people, an entity, a total concern whose components he would never think of dissociating. To point out this very elementary reality, Brecht then creates a new word, soldering together three old words. The invention is in no way gratuitous since it becomes inscribed in the logic of social relationships.

1 The twentieth-century French surrealist poet.

Brecht manages this logic, or rather dialectic, subtly. It is noticeable in the poem that the *I* does not refer to the poet. It is the oppressor who is speaking, but his words are constantly subject to criticism. They are accompanied, in muted tones, by the reactions of the oppressed or, at least, by the reactions that Brecht would like to suggest to the oppressed. Giving his voice to violence, he denounces its unavowed goals and indicates the way to resist it. He strips it of its fatal, irrational, and terrifying character. He revives a hope at the same time he seems to be forbidding all hope. And in this poem which affirms (in appearance) that nothing will ever change, he introduces contradiction, a microscopic "perhaps," an "if," a conditional. He does not say *werden* (*in das Zink kommen*), but *sollen*, thus transforming a fatality into will (of the class).[2] Now all will can imply a counter-will. So then, for the poverty of subjective lyricism, Brecht substitutes the complexity of an objective and social lyricism "in three voices": that of the oppressed, of the oppressor, and of the critic-poet. In fact, three wills come face to face in this poem, a faithful mirror of a moment of history. Obviously, it is no way a question of a thesis poem. The truth springs from an analysis of the real. But behind what *is*, the poet uncovers (and helps us to uncover) what is *to become of it*. In a word, his poetry is movement.

The same dialectic is found in a poem written in exile where Brecht answers the questions of his son: is it worth the trouble to learn history, French, mathematics in this time of ignorance and insecurity? Even there three voices come face to face: that—interrogative—of the son, and those—contradictory—of the father. One expresses a shortsighted realism, and the other puts its confidence, in an almost insensate fashion, in the future. The poem depicts and clarifies an elementary social relationship (father to son). It is intercourse, dialogue, and an interplay of questions and answers, all in all a common effort to gain a certainty. And this certainty, which is deserved because it is earned, breaks through in the last two lines where the harmony

2 The exact translation would be: "ought to be put in a zinc shroud" and not "will be put."

between the father and the son is finally proclaimed: "Yes, learn mathematics, I tell you, learn history and learn French!"

Thus, maturity answers the questions of youth. Is harmony possible? Yes, but in the bosom of discord. In his poetic testament, "To Posterity," Brecht defined this paradox:

> Willingly, I too would be wise.
> The old books tell us what wisdom is:
> Holding ourselves aloof from the conflicts of this world and
>   without terror
> Living out the little time which is meted out to us,
> Using no violence, returning evil
> With good, not following our desires,
> Forgetting them. There we have
> What passes for wisdom,
> But all that, I can't do it.
> Really, what a sad century we live in!

And yet the poem ends on a note of hope. Brecht gives us a glimpse of a time "when at last it comes to pass/That man can help his fellow man." The final elegies, which he composed in the summer of 1953, during a vacation at Buchow, go beyond Brechtian irony. In them he dreams of showing men "agreeable things." There the contradictions of the world are resolved in an abundance of water and greenery. The poetry is happy, although on the edge of danger.

> It is evening. One can see, sliding over the water,
> Two canoes each of which bear
> A nude young man. Rowing side by side
> They converse. Conversing
> They row side by side.

We imagine some Anacreontic harmony, but we are going to see the difference. Anacreon shows us man at rest, thus completing the antique tragedy, which is discord and conflict. Now Brecht surmounts this opposition. With him, the harmony is an integral part of the battle. It is not born, as with Anacreon, from the intoxication by wine. It is no longer solitary or passive.

> The little house under the trees by the side of the lake,
> Has smoke rising from its roof.
> If it happened to be lacking,

> Then how desolate would be
> The house and the trees and the lake.

Anacreon remains removed from the works of men: he contemplates. Brecht participates; he even makes the poem surge forth from the works of men. The harmony that he proposes is the fruit of a competition. It is an intelligent harmony. Anacreon eulogizes "the unbroken mare"; his harmony is Dionysiac. He is alone before nature and upon it he projects his gods. Brecht does not dream; he marks nature with his imprint. He does not do it alone but in common action with other men. His song is no longer cut off from action, it is action itself.

This beginning of harmony remains critical. Certain of Brecht's posthumous poems openly reveal his political reserves on the subject. They show very exactly just what is opposed, for the time being, to a harmony with no reservations. Is that to say, as some suggest, that Brecht, toward the end of his life, ceased to believe in it? Until the last day we see him dissociating the old from the new. Would he be doing that if he had no hope in the future? As I examine the last portraits of Brecht, I see in them signs of a wounded kindness, of fatigue above all, and of few illusions. But there is nothing in them, it seems to me, that could make one think of despair. Death was already gnawing at him. His heart was breaking from having fought and hoped too much.

> People's strength was lacking and the goal
> lay very far in the distance.
> It was clearly visible, but as for me,
> I scarcely believed that I could attain it.
> That's how time has passed,
> The time that was given to me on earth.

Chronology

"IT IS NOT yourselves but the world you must present," wrote Brecht in a poem which he addressed to actors. He himself followed this directive. His works are poor in personal confidences, and today one can scarcely find an author more bent on fleeing public indiscretion. With the exception of a brief fragment published in *Sinn und Form* (1957), his work journal remains unpublished. Only its complete publication will permit a critical, probing study of the mental workings of Brecht. At the same time, it will also correct the hesitations, approximations, and lacunae of contemporary biographies. Among these, the most complete are those by Marianne Kesting, Kurt Fassmann, and John Willett (Methuen, London). We have taken these into account. Brecht's works are mentioned the year that he finished them. In parentheses are the years when he probably started to work on them.

1898—2/10: Born Berthold Eugen Friedrich Brecht in Augsburg. Father: Berthold Brecht, director of a paper factory; mother: Sophie, née Brezing.

1904–1908—Elementary school.

1908–1917—Secondary school at Augsburg.

1914—Publishes, under the pseudonym of Berthold Eugen, his first poems and narratives in the *Augsburger Neueste Nachrichten.*

1915—As the result of a pacifist dissertation, he is almost expelled from school.

1917—Graduates and begins his medical studies.

1918—Arranges a tribute to Wedekind in a Munich tavern. Drafted into a military hospital at Augsburg. At the end of the war he returns to study in Munich. Follower of the Independent Social-Democrat Party. (*Baal*)

1919—Makes the acquaintance of Lion Feuchtwanger and Johannes Becher. February–March: takes part in the Spartakist agitation. Elected to the Council of Workers and Soldiers of Augsburg. Theater critic for *Der Volkswille* (Communist) until the end of 1920. Plays in the cabarets of Trude Hesterberg and Karl Valentin.

1920—1/15: Death of his mother. Settles in Munich. Becomes attached to Blandine Ebinger. Friendship with Carola Neher and Erich Engel, his future collaborators. (*Drums in the Night*—1919)

1921—First contacts at Berlin. Publishes some narratives in *Der neue Merkur* (Munich). Writes four one-act plays, influenced by the popular comic Karl Valentin. (*The Beggar, He Expels the Devil, Lux in Tenebris, The Wedding*—unpublished)

1922—Second trip to Berlin where he meets Arnolt Bronnen, a member of the extreme right. Spells his first name "Bertholt." 9/23: Premiere of *Drums in the Night* at Munich. Herbert Ihering obtains the Kleist Prize for him. 11/3: Marriage to the singer Josephine Zoff. Outlines for a play on Hannibal. 12/20: *Drums in the Night* presented at the Deutsches Theater in Berlin. (*In the Cities' Jungle*—1921)

1923—3/12: Birth of his daughter Hanne Marianne. 5/9: Premiere of *In the Cities' Jungle* at Munich. Hired by the Pocket Theater of the same city, which entrusts him with the production of *Macbeth*. After the *Putsch* of Munich, Hitler and Ludendorff list him among the suspects to be arrested. December: Premiere of *Baal* in Leipzig. (*Edward II*, from Marlowe's play in collaboration with Feuchtwanger)

1924—3/18: Munich premiere of *Edward II*, produced by Brecht himself. Moves to Berlin; hired, along with Karl Zuckmayer,

by Max Reinhardt. Meets Helene Weigel. *In the Cities'
Jungle* and *Edward II* produced in Berlin.

1925—Writes for several Berlin papers. Becomes friendly with
the boxer Paul Samson Körner and the satiric artist, George
Grosz. (*A Man's a Man*—1924)

1926—Produces *Baal* at Berlin. Premiere of *A Man's a Man*
(9/26, Darnstadt) and of *The Wedding* (12/1, Frankfort).
(*Taschenpostille*, private edition)

1927—Publishes *Hauspostille* in Berlin. Works at Piscator's
theater (where *Schwejk* by Hasek is staged). Studies Marxism.
7/17: Presents with Kurt Weill, *Little Mahagonny* at the
Baden-Baden festival. 11/22: Divorce.

1928—1/5: Premiere of *A Man's a Man* at the Volksbühne in
Berlin. 8/31: Premiere of *The Threepenny Opera* at the Schiffbauerdamm. From this time, Brecht has at his disposal his
own theater. Marries Helene Weigel. The critic Alfred Kerr
accuses him of having plagiarized François Villon.

1929—Presents *Lindbergh's Flight* and the *Didactic Play for
Baden-Baden*. Stages *Happy End* (in collaboration with
Elisabeth Hauptmann) at the Schiffbauerdamm.

1930—Premieres of *Mahagonny* (3/9, Leipzig) and of *The Decision* (12/10, Berlin) which causes a scandal. Publishes his
first two notebooks of *Versuche* at Kiepenheuer. May: Con-
valescence at Lavendou (France), then takes a cure at a Ba-
varian sanatorium. 10/18: Birth of his daughter Maria
Barbara. (*St. Joan of the Stockyards*, 1929; *Rise and Fall of
the Town of Mahagonny*, 1928; *The Exception and the Rule,
He Who Said Yes*, and *He Who Said No*, 1929; theoretical
writings)

1931—Premiere of *A Man's a Man* (second version) in Berlin.
After Brecht had been eliminated by the producers, Pabst
alone makes a film taken from *The Threepenny Opera*.
Adaptation of *Hamlet* for the radio. Edits the scenario for a
socialist film by Dudow: *Kuhle Wampe*. Exhibition forbidden.

1932—1/15: Premiere of *The Mother* (adapted from Gorki,
1930) at the Schiffbauerdamm. *St. Joan* presented by Radio

Berlin. (*The Three Soldiers*, a book for children with drawings by Grosz)

1933—1/28: Performance of *The Decision* interrupted by the Erfurt police. Sought for high treason. 2/28: The day following the fire at the Reichstag, Brecht flees Germany with his family and some friends. Prague, Vienna, Zurich. April–September: Holiday at Carona in the Tessin. Meets Hermann Hesse. 5/10: Nazis burn Brecht's books. June: *The Seven Deadly Sins* (of the petty bourgeois) presented by Balanchine at the Champs-Elysées. Lotte Lenya (Weill's wife) plays the singing role. Brief trip to Paris, then Copenhagen. Moves to a farm at Swedenborg (Denmark). (*Round Heads and Pointed Heads*, 1932)

1934—Collaborates on the refugees' newspapers. November–December: In London with the composer Hans Eisler. (*The Threepenny Novel*, 1933; *The Horatii and the Curiatii*)

1935—6/8: Loses German citizenship. June: Speech at the International Congress of Writers (Paris). November–February: New York. Attends the American premiere of *The Mother* (Civic Repertory Theater). (*Five Difficulties*)

1936—*The Seven Deadly Sins* has only one performance in Copenhagen. Works for Lukacs' review (*Internationale Literatur*, Moscow) and becomes the editor of Feuchtwanger's review (*Das Wort*, Moscow). November: Production of *Round Heads* in Copenhagen. Writes on the Chinese theater.

1937—9/28: *The Threepenny Opera* with Yvette Guilbert at the Théâtre de l'Etoile (Paris). October: Stages *Señora Carrar's Rifles* in Paris. Begins a novel (never completed): *Tui*.

1938—5/21: Helene Weigel acts some scenes from *Terror and Misery in the Third Reich* in Paris. Meets Martin Andersen-Nexö at Copenhagen.

1939—5/12: Attends the London congress of émigrés. 5/20: Death of his father. July: Pierre Abraham stages *Terror and Misery* in Paris. (*The Life of Galileo*, first version, 1938; *The Good Woman of Setzuan*, 1938; *The Trial of Lucullus*; *Mother Courage*; *Poems of Swedenborg*)

1940—April: Nazi armies invade Denmark; Brecht takes refuge in Finland. Guest of the writer Hella Wuolijoki.

1941—4/19: Premiere of *Mother Courage* at Zurich. May–June: German divisions penetrate into Finland. Brecht and his family cross the U.S.S.R. and reach California. Buys a house near Hollywood. Reunited with Feuchtwanger, Fritz Lang, Hans Eisler, Paul Dessau, Heinrich Mann, Leonhard Frank. Friendly wtih Aldous Huxley and Charlie Chaplin. (*Herr Puntila*, 1940; *Arturo Ui*)

1942—Meets Schönberg; collaborates on films by Eric Bentley, Fritz Lang, Vladimir Pozner.

1943—Premieres of *The Good Woman* (2/4) and *The Life of Galileo* (9/9) at Zurich. February: A short stay with Piscator in New York. Outlines with Dessau *The Voyages of the Good God*, an unfinished opera. *The Threepenny Novel* published in New York. (*The Visions of Simone Machard*, 1941; *The Good Soldier Schweik in the Second World War*, 1941)

1945—*Terror and Misery* presented in San Francisco and New York. (*The Caucasian Chalk Circle*, 1944)

1946—With Charles Laughton he develops a second version (English) of *The Life of Galileo*.

1947—*Terror and Misery* staged in Berlin. 7/31: Premiere of *The Life of Galileo*, produced by Brecht and Losey, at the Coronet Theater (Hollywood). In December the play is done in New York. October: Questioned by the Un-American Activities Committee in Washington. November: Leaves the United States for Switzerland. (*Antigone*, from the plays of Sophocles and Hölderlin)

1948—Settles near Zurich. Becomes friendly with Max Frisch; meets Gunther Weisenborn again. February: Premiere of *Antigone* at Coire. 6/5: Premiere of *Puntila* in Zurich. Occupation authorities refuse him a visa to East Germany. Obtains a Czech passport and reaches East Berlin via Prague. Put in charge of the Deutsches Theater. (*Kalendergeschichten*, *A Little Organum*)

1949—Stages *Mother Courage* (1/11) and *Puntila* (11/12) at
the Deutsches Theater. September: with Helene Weigel he
founds the Berliner Ensemble. (*The Days of the Commune*,
1948; *The Business Deals of Mr. Julius Caesar*, fragment of
a novel)

1950—4/12: Brecht and his wife obtain Austrian citizenship.
Named member of the Academy of Arts (East Berlin). The
State loans him a villa at Buchow. (*The Preceptor*, adapted
from Lenz)

1951—3/17: Premiere of *The Trial of Lucullus*, with music by
Paul Dessau. Criticized by the Party. Brecht agrees to rework
certain details and change the title ("condemnation" instead
of "trial"). August: *Herrenburger Bericht* presented at the
World Festival of Youth (East Berlin). 10/7: Receives the
First Class National Prize. The Berliner Ensemble presents
Señora Carrar's Rifles and *The Mother*. Open letters to
German artists and writers, as at the World Council of Peace.
(*Die Erziehung der Hirse, Theater-arbeit*)

1952—February: The Berliner Ensemble in Warsaw. (*Don
Juan*, adapted from the play by Molière, *The Trial of Joan of
Arc*, adapted from the play by Anna Seghers)

1953—January: Telegrams to Albert Einstein, Arthur Miller,
and Ernest Hemingway for clemency for the Rosenbergs.
May: Elected president of the East Berlin PEN. 6/17: Open
letter to Ulbricht on the workers' uprising in East Berlin.
With only the last sentence having been published, addresses
a second message to Ulbricht (6/21). Moves into Chaussee-
strasse. (*Coriolanus*, adapted from the play by Shakespeare,
1952; *Elegies for Buchow*)

1954—March: The Berliner Ensemble moves to Schiffbauer-
damm. 6/15: Premiere of *The Caucasian Chalk Circle*. July:
The Berliner Ensemble presents *Mother Courage* at the Festi-
val of Paris and wins the first prize. December: With Johannes
Becher, Brecht attends a meeting of intellectuals from both
Germanies (West Berlin). (*Turandot or the Laundrymen's
Congress*, 1953)

1955—January: The Berliner Ensemble presents one of Becher's plays. Trip to Moscow, where he receives the Stalin Prize. 2/12: Intervenes for the "Partisans of Peace" (Dresden). March: Attends the congress of PEN (Hamburg). 5/15: Testament-letter to the Academy of Arts of East Berlin. July: The Berliner Ensemble presents *The Caucasian Chalk Circle* at the second Festival of Paris. Purchases a house on the Danish coast. (*Drums and Trumpets*, adapted from Farquhar; *The ABC of War*)

1956—January: Intervention at the Fourth Congress of German Writers. Catches influenza and is hospitalized. 7/4: Letter to the Bonn Bundestag against German rearmament. 8/10: In spite of his feeble health he attends a performance of *Galileo*. 8/14: At 11:45 P.M. he dies at his home of an infarct. 8/17: Buried near Hegel in the Dorotheenfriedhof which his workroom overlooked. 8/18: Ceremony at the Berliner Ensemble with speeches by Georg Lukacs, Johannes Becher, Walter Ulbricht.

Bibliography

WALTER NUBEL has undertaken a scientific bibliography of all the writings by and about Brecht. The fragments which he presented in the second special number of *Sinn und Form* concern only publications in the German language and stop at 1956, but they take up no less than 140 pages. Bernard Dort made an effort to complete these bibliographical fragments, though in a provisional and partial fashion, with the articles and works published in English and French. Any choice will remain arbitrary, and for this reason, we have left out all the articles scattered throughout numerous periodicals. Since most of Brecht's works have gone through many editions, we have been careful to indicate only those which are most convenient and easy to obtain.

WORKS OF BRECHT IN GERMAN
Versuche (Suhrkamp, Berlin).
1–4. Ozeanflug; Radiotheorie; Keuner; Fatzer, 3; Mahagonny; Lesebuch für Städtebewohner; Badener Lehrstück; Dreigroschenoper, film, prozess; Jasager und Neinsager; Massnahme.

5–8. Heilige Johanna der Schlachthöfe; Keuner; Drei Soldaten; Geschichten aus der Revolution; Spitzköpfe und Rundköpfe.

9. Mutter Courage; Fünf Schwierigkeiten beim Schreiben der Wahrheit.

10. Puntila; Anmerkungen zum Volksstück; Strassenszene; Chinesische Gedichte; Ausnahme und Regel.

11. Hofmeister; Studien; Neue Technik der Schauspielkunst; Uebungs stücke für Schauspieler; Verhör des Lukullus.

12. Gute Mensch von Sezuan; Kleines Organon; Ueber reimlose Lyrik; Keuner.

13. Kaukasische Kreidekreis; Weite und Vielfalt der realistischen Schreibweise; Buckower Elegien.

14. Leben des Galilei; Gedichte aus dem Messingkauf; Horatier und Kuriatier.

15. Tage der Commune; Dialektik auf dem Theater; Zum "Leben des Galilei"; Drei Reden, drei Briefe.

Stücke (Suhrkamp, Berlin).

1. Bei Durchsicht meiner ersten Stücke; Baal; Trommeln in der Nacht; Im Dickicht der Städte.

2. Eduard der II. (nach Marlowe); Mann ist Mann.

3. Dreigroschenoper; Mahagonny; Badener Lehrstück.

4. Heilige Johanna der Schlachthöfe; Jasager und Neinsager; Massnahme.

5. Mutter (nach Gorki); Ausnahme und Regel; Horatier und Kuriatier; Anmerkung zu den Lehrstücken.

6. Rundköpfe und Spitzköpfe; Furcht und Elend des III. Reiches.

7. Gewehre der Frau Carrar; Mutter Courage; Verhör des Lukullus.

8. Leben des Galilei; Gute Mensch von Sezuan.

9. Puntila; Aufhaltsame Aufstieg des Arturo Ui; Gesichte der Simone Machard.

10. Schweyk im zweiten Weltkrieg; Kaukasische Kreidekreis; Tage der Commune.

11. Antigone des Sophokles; Hofmeister (nach Lenz); Coriolan (nach Shakespeare).

12. Prozess der Jeanne d'Arc (nach Anna Seghers); Don Juan (nach Molière); Pauken und Trompeten (nach Farquhar).

Die Erziehund der Hirse, Henschel, Berlin.
Taschenpostille, Aufbau, Berlin.
Hauspostille, Suhrkamp, Berlin.
Hundert Gedichte 1918–1950, Aufbau, Berlin.
Herrnburger Bericht, Neues Leben, Berlin.
Gedichte und Lieder, Suhrkamp, Berlin.
Lieder und Gesänge, Henschel, Berlin.
Dreigroschenroman, Rowohlt, Hamburg.
Kalendergeschicten, Rowohlt, Berlin.
Kriegsfibel, Eulenspiegel, Berlin.
Die Geschäfte des Herrn Julius Caesar, Weiss, Berlin.
Schriften zum Theater, Suhrkamp, Berlin.
Theaterarbeit, Sechs Aufführungen des Berliner Ensembles, VVV Dresdener Verlag, Dresden.
Antigonenmodell 1948, Henschel, Berlin.
Modellbuch Galilei, Henschel, Berlin.
Modellbuch Courage, Henschel, Berlin.

WORKS OF BRECHT IN ENGLISH

Bentley, E. *et al. Seven Plays by Bertolt Brecht.* New York: Grove Press, 1961.

Bentley, E. and M. *Parables for the Theatre.* Minnesota and Oxford, 1948.

(The first volume of a collection of Brecht's plays in translation has been published by Methuen.)

Bertolt Brecht, Selected Poems. Tr. H. R. Hays. Evergreen Books, Grove Press, and John Calder, London, 1959. (First published in 1947.)

A *Penny for the Poor.* Tr. D. I. Vesey and C. Isherwood. London, 1937.

Reprinted as *Threepenny Novel,* Grove Press, New York, 1956.

(These translations are the easiest to obtain. It seems redundant to list all the translations of plays, poems, and works of dramatic theory which are to be found in obscure reviews. The bibliographies of Willett, Esslin, and Gray cover the subject more than adequately.)

WRITINGS ON BRECHT IN GERMAN

Sinn und Form, special numbers in 1949 and 1957.

Schumacher, Ernst. *Die dramatischen Versuche Bertolt Brechts 1918–1933*, Rutten und Loening, Berlin.

Fassmann, Kurt, *Bert Brecht, eine Bildbiographie*, Kindler, Munchen.

Kesting, Marianne. *Bertolt Brecht*, Rowohlt, Hamburg.

Ihering, Herbert. *Bertolt Brecht und das Theater*, Rembrandt, Berlin.

Klotz, Volker. *Bertolt Brecht, Versuch über sein Werk*, Genter, Darmstadt.

To these basic works, the recent studies by Walter Hinck, Reinhold Grimm, Willy Haas, and Gerhard Zwerens can be added. For articles which have appeared since 1956, see Marianne Kesting.

WRITINGS ON BRECHT IN ENGLISH AND FRENCH

Dort, Bernard. *Lecture de Brecht*, Paris: Seuil, 1960.

Esslin, Martin. *Brecht, a Choice of Evils*. London: 1959.

Gray, Ronald. *Bertolt Brecht*. New York: Grove, 1961.

Serreau, Geneviève. *Brecht*. Paris: L'Arbre, 1955.

Willett, John. *The Theatre of Bertolt Brecht*. London, 1959.

Wintzen, René. *Bertolt Brecht*. Paris: Seghers, 1954.

Index